SOFTWARE AS CAPITAL

AN ECONOMIC PERSPECTIVE
ON SOFTWARE ENGINEERING

Howard Baetjer, Jr.

Program on Social and Organizational Learning
George Mason University

IEEE
COMPUTER
SOCIETY

Los Alamitos, California

Washington • Brussels • Tokyo

Library of Congress Cataloging-in-Publication Data

Baetjer, Howard.
   Software as capital: an economic perspective on software engineering /
Howard Baetjer.
      p.   cm.
   Includes bibliographical references and index.
   ISBN 0-8186-7779-1
   1. Software engineering—Economic aspects.   I. Title.
QA76.758.B34   1998
338.4 ' 5610053—dc21

                                                            97-38111
                                                               CIP

IEEE Computer Society Press Order Number BP07779
Library of Congress Number 97-38111
ISBN 0-8186-7779-1

Additional copies may be ordered from:

IEEE Computer Society Press
Customer Service Center
10662 Los Vaqueros Circle
P.O. Box 3014
Los Alamitos, CA 90720-1314
Tel: +1-714-821-8380
Fax: +1-714-821-4641
Email: cs.books@computer.org

IEEE Service Center
445 Hoes Lane
P.O. Box 1331
Piscataway, NJ 08855-1331
Tel: +1-732-981-0060
Fax: +1-732-981-9667
mis.custserv@computer.org

IEEE Computer Society
Watanabe Building
1-4-2 Minami-Aoyama
Minato-ku, Tokyo 107-0062
JAPAN
Tel: +81-3-3408-3118
Fax: +81-3-3408-3553
tokyo.ofc@computer.org

Publisher: Matt Loeb
Developmental Editor: Cheryl Baltes
Advertising/Promotions: Tom Fink
Cover Design: Walzak Advertising and Design, Inc.
Printed in the United States of America by BookCrafters

For Don, Bill, Kevin, and Mark M.

CONTENTS

PREFACE

How does an economist come to write a book on software development? The process began with the dissertation I wrote for my Ph.D. in economics at George Mason University in 1992 and 1993. This book has grown out of that dissertation. My general goal in that research was to understand better the nature of economic development. More particularly, believing that better, more productive tools and processes—capital goods—are responsible for the lion's share of economic development in all times and places, I wanted to understand the process of building new tools and improving them over time. I chose to study the software industry for reasons I'll describe below.

The research went well. In looking at the software development process and the way its tools and methodologies have evolved, I learned much about economic evolution and refined my understanding of my own favorite branch of economics, capital theory.

I also learned a fair amount about software development as such, and gained some insights into why the software industry has evolved as it has, what kinds of software development tools and processes usually work better than others, and what the industry in general needs in order to take a quantum leap forward in productive power. In short, I thought I had some useful things to say to the software industry, from my perspective as a capital theorist of the "Austrian School." Hence this book.

• • •

Why would an economist seeking to understand how better capital goods contribute to economic development focus on software development?

It is because knowledge is prominent in software as in no other type of capital good. Following the great Austrian economist Carl Menger, I view capital goods as being fundamentally embodied knowledge. This book emphasizes this view, and strives to explicate the processes by which knowledge is elicited, discovered, and embodied in the capital structure. With most other kinds of capital goods it is easy to overlook how much knowledge is built into them, because what we see is the steel and glass, the copper and plastic, the silicon and polymer in which that knowledge is embedded. Software, by contrast, we do not see at all; we think about it independent of its physical form. We are equally comfortable thinking about it as printed out on paper, stored magnetically on a floppy disk, or loaded and running in the circuits of a computer. Indifferent to the physical medium in which it is embodied, we are readily able to focus on the knowledge that software embodies.

While the book focuses on software, the principles discussed apply to capital goods in general. All kinds of capital goods are embodied knowledge; the essence of all of them is knowledge, not the physical substrate on which that knowledge is imprinted. Readers are invited to extrapolate beyond software as they read, looking for parallels to physical capital.

The first chapter lays the theoretical foundation for the investigation, drawing on Austrian capital theory for understanding of the relationships between knowledge and capital, and of the structural aspects of capital. It argues that, given the nature of capital goods, capital development is inevitably a social learning process. Chapter 2 then provides an overview of the history and terminology of software development, introducing some of the main issues which subsequent chapters will investigate for illumination of this process.

Chapter 3 discusses initial software development, looking particularly at the evolution of the procedures and tools used. It demonstrates that software development, like all capital goods development, is a process of interactive, social learning. Accordingly, the development process should be tuned to support social learning. Chapter 4 investigates the on-going development of software—software maintenance. Because capital structures are always evolving, the software itself needs to be tuned for evolvability. The chapter assesses the characteristics of software which is able to evolve readily. Modularity is fundamentally important, primarily because of the way it enhances understandability.

Chapter 5 broadens the perspective to examine the main failing of the software industry as compared to other industries: the absence of an extensive division of labor supported by markets for software components. It sets out the reasons for this problem, an outline of its solution, and the benefits that will result when and if the problem is solved. Chapter 6 summarizes the whole.

Finally, Appendix A points out that the neoclassical growth theory of mainstream economics offers little insight into the role of capital in economic development. Appendix B briefly indicates that the general principles of good software development discussed in the book apply closely to hard tools as well.

ACKNOWLEDGMENTS

I am grateful to the Center for Market Processes at George Mason University for the generous financial, intellectual, and emotional support that made this book possible. I am grateful as well to the Claude R. Lambe Foundation and the J. M. Foundation for financial support.

Kent Beck and Ward Cunningham each provided an extremely valuable interview: many thanks to them both. Thanks to Tom Wrensch for helping me learn Smalltalk and understand better the software development process. I am also indebted to Paul Ambrose, Lee Griffin of IBM, Richard Collum of First Union National Bank of North Carolina, and Bill Waldron of Krautkamer Branson for short, but valuable, conversations about the software development process.

Thanks to Phil Salin, founder of the American Information Exchange Corp., and to all my teammates at AMiX, with whom I shared the experience of trying to bootstrap an electronic market for software components. I am grateful to Dr. Brad Cox for his steady support of my work, well before he joined my dissertation committee, and for the continuing inspiration of his fertile mind and stubborn persistence.

Thanks to Karen Vaughn for her thorough reading and thoughtful criticism of the dissertation.

Thanks to Mark S. Miller and K. Eric Drexler for opening my eyes to this general area of research, and to Mark in particular for extensive interviews, inspiration, and support.

Thanks to Kevin Lacobie for research help and for numerous valuable discussions.

I am very grateful to Bill Tulloh for a host of valuable suggestions and insights into this topic, for inestimable help with research, for criticism of earlier drafts, and for his enthusiasm for the topic.

Thanks to my wife, Susan, for her calm, patient support during the rewriting process.

My primary debt of gratitude is to my dissertation chairman and now colleague, Don Lavoie. For his steady support and encouragement, for intellectual inspiration, for his generosity in time, attention, and timely response to every request for guidance, and in particular for the example of his passion for understanding, I am extremely grateful.

Knowledge Capital and Economic Growth

Men, my brothers, men, the workers, ever reaping something new,
That which they have done but earnest of the things that they shall do.

For I dipped into the future, far as human eye could see,
Saw the Vision of the world, and all the wonder that would be.

—Tennyson, "Locksley Hall"

BETTER TOOLS INCREASE
THE WEALTH OF NATIONS

The research underpinning this book was motivated by the same question that motivated the first great book on economics, *An Inquiry into the Nature and Causes of the Wealth of Nations*, by the "father of economics," Adam Smith, published in 1776. The question: how do we account for human beings' economic advancement? How is it that our race of talking primates has been able to advance from barbarism to abundance (at least in certain areas of the world)? What is the nature of the process by which we are able, over time, to get more and better of the "necessaries and conveniencies of life," as Smith put it, for the same amount of effort?

Economists agree on the broad answer to that question: we advance in economic well-being in three main ways. The two more apparent of these are:

- increasing productivity per person, and
- extending trade.

These depend on another, more foundational element:

- evolving appropriate social rules of just conduct.

1

By increasing productivity per person, we generate more goods with a given effort; by extending trade, we share those goods among ourselves in a more satisfying way. Appropriate social rules of just conduct make the first two possible: to the extent that a society has reasonably well-articulated and enforced standards of promise keeping (sanctity of contract), respect for the possessions of others (private property), and equal treatment of all (the rule of law), productivity can increase and trade can expand.

We will focus on the first of these three requirements for improving well-being and ask, *how does a society improve its productivity,* its ability to produce more of the things it wants with a given amount of human effort? A moment's reflection suggests how important a question this is: Through most of human history, and in much of the world today, most people suffered hard physical labor every day of a short life to produce subsistence amounts of food, clothing, and shelter. We in the modern developed West work fewer hours, with our minds or with machines for the physical work, in comfortable conditions; yet we produce an abundance of luxuries unknown to kings and queens of old—hot and cold running water, music at the touch of a switch, fresh fruit in midwinter. When our nation began, a couple of centuries ago, it took 75 percent of the population to produce enough food for all. Today it takes less than 3 percent of our population to feed all of us and many in other lands. What makes these wonders possible? *How does a society become so productive?*

It does so by increasing its knowledge of productive relationships and building this knowledge into better tools—better devices which extend people's physical, perceptual, and mental faculties for producing things we want.[1] This book is about the dual process of increasing our knowledge and building it into better tools.

---

[1] This view of human advancement derives from the "Austrian School of economics," to which I commend my computer-science audience, and in particular from the founder of the Austrian School, Carl Menger. I believe those interested in object-oriented programming will find "Austrian economics" especially agreeable. Indeed, one of my colleagues pronounces with a smile that "F. A. Hayek was the first object-oriented programmer." Hayek, pre-eminent in the Austrian School, was Nobel Laureate in economics in 1974. Essential works in this tradition are Menger (1871), Bohm-Bawerk (1889), Hayek (1935 and 1941), Mises (1966), and Lachmann (1978).

Of course, we may improve productivity by working harder, but the effect of greater exertion is far less than the effect of using better tools. In a task such as reaping grain, for example, even the most heroically increased exertions of a barehanded reaper yield far smaller productivity gains than merely using a steel sickle. Also, we may improve productivity by producing greater numbers of the same kinds of tools, but here again the effects fall far short of the effects of building better tools. Even if we were to equip everyone in the village with a steel sickle, productivity at harvest time would fall far short of what it would be if we were to equip only one worker with a John Deere grain combine. Better tools, then, are the key to greater productivity. For a society to improve its productivity, that society must improve the quality of its tools—its capital goods.

We use capital goods in production, which is a matter of transforming our condition from a less-preferred to more-preferred state. Lacking divine power to create something from nothing, when we produce we are really rearranging physical stuff into a form we prefer. What transformations will answer our purposes, and how to carry them out, are the crucial questions. Any capital good, any "produced means of production," is going to be some kind of embodied knowledge of what to do and how. Capital goods, then, are saved-up learning which helps us produce.

How does a society improve the quality of its capital goods? In what manner do we manage to generate and "save up" new knowledge of useful transformations? What is the nature of the process, and what is involved in the process? These questions will be explored in what follows.

THE EVOLVING CAPITAL STRUCTURE

Because I am a social scientist writing for a software engineering audience, there is a danger that I'll assume my readers understand what I mean by certain terms, when in fact they don't. With that in mind, let us step back a moment and consider an extended illustration of the essential economic concept that provides context for everything else I will discuss in this book. That concept is *evolving capital structure*.

When economists speak in general of the "capital structure"—sometimes known as "the structure of production"—we mean that complex and far-flung pattern of interacting tools, processes, and raw and intermediate goods that people use in producing things. This pattern or network, very like a vast ecosystem of overlapping food chains, is constantly evolving, as the people within it develop new tools, processes, and the corresponding raw and intermediate goods to feed them. There are two key points to keep in mind, which the following example is intended to illustrate: a) The system as a whole is complex beyond comprehension. b) The system is constantly in flux, constantly evolving.

In order to begin to appreciate the evolving capital structure, and to make sure that I will be understood when I speak of it, let us consider one change in one piece of it, which I happened to observe in the late 1970s.

We begin with milk on the breakfast table. Milk is a "consumption good" because we consume it directly when we drink it or pour it over our cereal.[2] As a consumption good, milk is one of those goods that the capital structure exists to produce. The whole point of the capital structure, after all, is to produce for us the things we want to consume or otherwise enjoy.

The milk on our breakfast table is itself the result of a long, complex production process, in which many tools, processes, raw, and intermediate goods are used. All those tools, processes, raw, and intermediate goods constitute "the milk capital structure," or the structure of production of milk. Let us trace a part of it.

We note in passing the grocery store building and refrigeration where we bought the milk (and all the bricks and mortar, compressors, and refrigerants involved there, as well as all the tools and materials that went into producing *them*). We keep in mind the delivery trucks, the dairy (and the paper mills that made the milk cartons and the logging tools used in harvesting the trees that

---

[2] Actually, it is not necessarily this simple. Milk is sometimes a part of the capital structure, when it is an input to the production of something else, such as an omelet. In such cases, it is part of the means of production of an omelet. Evidently, then, what we consider to be consumption goods and what production goods (capital goods) depends on our aim—what we are thinking of as the goal of production.

became the paper), the pasteurizer, and the milking machines. We acknowledge the cow herself, of course. All of these, and all of the tools and processes that produce or support them, comprise parts of the capital structure for milk. If we were to attempt to trace the capital structure involved in the production of milk, we would have to trace *all* of these various contributing streams of intermediate goods and the tools that operate on them. Clearly, it is not possible for anyone to comprehend, or even be aware of more than a small portion of this endlessly ramifying structure at any one time.

The cow needs hay to eat through the winter months. The high-producing cows at the premium dairies eat prime alfalfa hay. How is alfalfa produced on a large scale? Of course, there are cutting machines, or swathers; there are balers to bale the hay, machines called harobeds that pick up the bales and stack them, and there are the trucks that carry the bales from the hayfields to the dairies. All these are part of the capital structure that puts milk on our tables. But, before the hay grows, at least on the big ranches in Lovelock, Nevada where I was a hired hand a couple of summers, the fields have to be irrigated.

Their irrigation water comes from the Humboldt River, which flows from the Ruby Mountains down to the Carson Sink, where what is left of it evaporates in the Nevada sun. Along the way, ranchers divert it into irrigation ditches and irrigate by letting the water flow into the high end of a gently sloped field. Irrigation ditches are thus part of the capital structure for milk. If the field is fairly flat, and sloped at the right pitch for the soil type, the water flows out evenly over most of it. But, of course, fields don't come naturally sloped and perfectly flat, so there is always work to do to get irrigation water to soak a whole field evenly.

Until the late 1970s, they channeled the water in the fields with levees, long mounds of dirt a couple of feet wide and about eighteen inches high. These ran the length of the fields, about twenty to thirty yards apart. When water was let into the fields through the sluice gates at the high end, these levees would channel the flow down the length of the field, preventing the water from running sideways too much. There was a special machine we would draw behind a tractor, called a levee builder, that built up and maintained the levees.

Of course, the levees were a nuisance. Alfalfa wouldn't grow on them because they didn't get any water, so their whole surface area was lost to the harvest. And, when harvest time came, the hands driving the swathers had to be careful neither to get so close to the levees as to damage them, nor to stay so far away that they missed hay along the edges (I know: I drove a swather one summer and I *hated* the levees).

By the next summer, however, the capital structure of alfalfa production (and hence of milk production) had evolved. The fields had been "laser-planed," and all the levees were gone. Here's how it worked: Skilled operators set up a laser on a rotating spindle at one end of the field. They calibrated it exactly so the plane of laser light it emitted sloped at exactly the inclination they wanted the field below it to have. Then they brought in the laser plane itself, a big machine with a large scraping blade at the bottom and a reservoir of good topsoil inside. At the top of this machine was a light sensor that would detect the laser. A system of electronics and hydraulics transmitted a signal from the laser sensor to the machinery in such a way that when the field sloped down slightly, causing the laser to strike a bit higher on the sensor, some topsoil would be pushed out of the reservoir. Conversely, when the field sloped up too high, the scraping blade would engage and shave it down.

With the lasers, electronics, and hydraulics set up properly, an unskilled hand could perfectly flatten and slope a 40-acre field by pulling the laser plane along behind a tractor, back and forth freely over the entire field. After laser planing, and without any levees, irrigation water released at the high end of a field at the right rate would flow out evenly and soak in to just the right depth over the whole field.

The effect on productivity was striking. No levees meant hay grew over every square inch of the field. There were no more minutes lost at harvest time as we slowed the swathers to make sure the levees weren't damaged and no more uncut strips along them where we stayed away to play it safe. There was no time spent repairing levees between growing cycles. Hay could now be produced more cheaply, meaning milk could be produced more cheaply.

Old tools and processes had been replaced by new and better: The capital structure had evolved. Maintaining evenness of irrigation with levees and levee builders had given way to doing so with laser planes. That part of the unimaginably extensive set of tools and processes that contribute to putting milk on our breakfast tables had changed for the better.

I have focused on the changeover from using levees to using laser planes only because I had first-hand experience with it. Undoubtedly, almost every other area of the structure of production of milk was evolving then, too, and has evolved continuously in the twenty years since I worked at the ranch. Swathers and balers are being improved, as are the trucks that ship the hay. The dairy is becoming more efficient, as is the grocery store and the refrigeration it uses. Capital structure evolution is a constant of our lives, though we may be blind to it or take its wonders for granted.

There is one other point to make before we leave this introductory example. That is, capital structure evolution usually involves increasing the complexity of the structure. When Nevada ranchers used levee builders to assure (relatively) even irrigation, they used a steel levee builder that operated on mechanical principles. When they went to laser planing, they used machines that incorporated advanced optics, chemistry, electronics, and hydraulics, as well as steel and mechanics. All the capital structure that went into building, calibrating, and producing lasers now became part of the capital structure of milk. The system became more complex. The pattern is similar in virtually all fields of enterprise: Improvements in productivity result from the capital structure evolving into increasingly complex and potent patterns of interaction.

CAPITAL GOODS AS KNOWLEDGE

To inform our examination of the process of capital development, we look in this section at capital itself. We will do so from the perspective of the Austrian School of economics. Unlike conventional, mainstream economics, Austrian economics stresses the role of knowledge in the economy, the importance of time and uncertainty, and the challenge of maintaining coordination among people with very different knowledge and purposes. (For a discussion of why mainstream theories of economic growth are unsuitable to this investigation, see Appendix A.)

There is a fundamental relationship between knowledge and capital. Indeed, capital *is* embodied knowledge of productive processes and how they may be carried out. Different varieties of knowledge are involved, as well as different kinds of embodiment.

EMBODIED KNOWLEDGE

Carl Menger, the first of the great Austrian economists, stresses the role of knowledge in human economic advancement. Fundamental to his thinking is that *knowledge is embodied in capital goods.* It is not enough just to understand physical laws and processes; we must apply this knowledge to tools and devices with which we can direct those processes to our purposes. He writes, "The quantities of consumption goods at human disposal are limited only by the extent of human knowledge of the causal connections between things, and by the extent of human control over these things" (1981, p. 74). To provide themselves with an ample supply of warm clothing, for example, early humans had to develop the knowledge that wool could be spun into yarn and the yarn woven into cloth. But further, if they were actually to have woolen clothing they had to apply this knowledge so as to "control" the wool: to spin it and weave it successfully into cloth. This knowledge of spinning and weaving they built into spinning machines and looms—capital goods for wool production.

In virtually all human production (other than gathering wild berries in open fields, and even there we often bring a pail or a box to carry them in), we employ capital goods—tools—for the purpose. Much of our knowledge of how to produce is found not in our heads, but in those capital goods that we employ. Capital is embodied knowledge.

In particular, capital equipment—tools of all kinds, including software—embodies knowledge of how to accomplish some purpose.3 Much of our knowledge of how to accomplish our purposes is not articulate but tacit. That is, we can do it, but we can't say in detail how we do it. In the beginning of *Wealth of Nations,* Adam Smith speaks of the "skill, dexterity, and judgment" (p. 7) of workers; these attributes are a kind of knowledge, a kinesthetic "knowledge" located in the hands rather than in the head. The improvements these skilled workers make in their tools are embodiments of that "knowledge." The very design of the tool passes on to a less skilled or dexterous worker the ability to accomplish the same results. Consider how the safety razor enables clumsy academics and engineers to shave with the blade always at the correct angle, rarely nicking ourselves. How well would we manage with straight razors? The skilled barber's dexterity has been passed on to us, as it were, embodied in the design of the safety razor.

Adam Smith gives a clear example of the embodiment of knowledge in capital equipment in his account of the development of early steam engines, on which:

> a boy was constantly employed to open and shut alternately the communication between the boiler and the cylinder, according as the piston either ascended or descended. One of those boys, who loved to play with his companions, observed that, by tying a string from the handle of the valve which opened this communication to another part of the machine, the valve would

---

3 Hayek writes

Take the concept of a "tool" or "instrument," or of any particular tool such as a hammer or a barometer. It is easily seen that these concepts cannot be interpreted to refer to "objective facts," that is, to things irrespective of what people think about them. Careful logical analysis of these concepts will show that they all express relationships between several (at least three) terms, of which one is the acting or thinking person, the second some desired or imagined effect, and the third a thing in the ordinary sense. If the reader will attempt a definition he will soon find that he cannot give one without using some term such as "suitable for" or "intended for" or some other expression referring to the use for which it is designed by somebody. And a definition which is to comprise all instances of the class will not contain any reference to its substance, or shape, or other physical attribute. An ordinary hammer and a steamhammer, or an aneroid barometer and a mercury barometer, have nothing in common except the purpose for which men think they can be used. (1979, p. 44)

open and shut without his assistance, and leave him at liberty
to divert himself with his playfellows. (p. 14)

The tying on of the string, and the addition of the metal rod
that was built on to subsequent steam engines to accomplish the
same purpose, is an archetypal case of the embodiment of knowledge in a tool. The boy's observation and insight were built into
the machine for use indefinitely into the future.

KNOWLEDGE IS OF THE ESSENCE

The point here is more radical than simply that capital goods have
knowledge in them. It is rather that capital goods *are knowledge,*
knowledge in the peculiar state of being embodied in such a form
that it is ready-to-hand for use in production. The knowledge
aspect of capital goods is the fundamental aspect. Any physical
aspect is incidental.

A hammer, for instance, is physical wood (the handle) and min-
erals (the head). But a piece of oak and a chunk of iron do not make
a hammer. The hammer is those raw materials plus all the knowledge required to shape the oak into a handle, to transform the iron
ore into a steel head, to shape it and fit it, and so on. There is a
great deal of knowledge embodied in the precise shape of the head
and handle, the curvature of the striking surface, the proportion of
head weight to handle length, and so on.

Even with a tool as bluntly physical as a hammer, the knowledge component is of overwhelming importance. With precision
tools such as microscopes and calibration instruments, the knowledge aspect of the tool becomes more dominant still. We might
say, imprecisely but helpfully, that there is a greater proportion of
knowledge to physical stuff in a microscope than in a hammer.

With computer software, on which we will turn our focus soon,
we have a logical extreme to inform further this approach to
understanding capital goods. Software is less tied to any physical
medium than most tools. Because we may with equal comfort
think of a given program as a program, whether it is printed out on
paper, stored on a diskette or tape, or loaded into the circuits of a
computer, we have no difficulty distinguishing the knowledge
aspect from the physical aspect of a software tool. Of course, to

function as a tool the software must be loaded and running in the physical medium of the computer, and there are definite physical limits to computation (Bennet 1985). Nevertheless, it is in the nature of computers and software to let us distinguish clearly the knowledge of how to accomplish a certain function from the physical embodiment of that knowledge.

The distinctness of the knowledge embodied in tools from the physical medium in which it is embodied was brought out humorously, years ago, in a remarkable exchange between two engineers working on a moon shot. One, (literally) a rocket scientist responsible for calculating propulsion capacity, approached the other, a software engineer. The rocket scientist wanted to know how to calculate the effect of all that software on the mass of the system. The software engineer didn't understand; was he asking about the weight of the computers? No, the computers' weight was already accounted for. Then what was the problem, asked the software engineer. "Well, you guys are using hundreds of thousands of lines of software in this moon shot, right?" "Right," said the software engineer. "Well," asked the rocket scientist, "how much does all that stuff weigh?" The reply: ". . . Nothing!!"[4]

Because the knowledge aspect of software tools is so clearly distinguishable from their physical embodiment, by investigating software capital we may distinguish clearly the knowledge aspects of capital in general. Although software may seem very different from other capital goods in this respect, when we think in terms of the capital structure, we find no fundamental difference between software tools and conventional tools. What is true of software is true of capital goods in general. What a person actually uses is not software alone, but software loaded into a physical system—a computer with a monitor, printer, or plotter; or space shuttle, or whatever. The computer is the multi-purpose, tangible complement to the special-purpose, intangible knowledge that is software. When a word-processing or CAD package is loaded in, the whole system can become a dedicated writing or drawing tool.

---

4 This story was told me in a personal conversation with Robert Polutchko of Martin Marietta Corporation.

But there is no conceptual difference in this respect between a word processor and a hammer. The oaken dowel and molten steel are the multi-purpose, tangible complements to the special-purpose, intangible knowledge of what a hammer is. When that knowledge is imprinted on the oak in the shape of a smooth, well-proportioned handle, and on the steel in the shape, weight, and hardness of a hammer-head, and when the two are joined together properly the whole system—raw oak, raw steel, and knowledge—becomes a dedicated nail-driving tool.

All tools are a combination of knowledge and matter. They are knowledge imprinted on or embodied in matter. Software is to the computer into which it is loaded as the knowledge of traditional tools is to the matter of which those tools are composed. As the circuits of the computer can be reprogrammed to other uses, so the physical stuff of the hammer can be taken apart and reformed for other purposes.

If this is true, then knowledge is the key aspect of all capital goods, because matter is, and always has been, "there." As Bohm-Bawerk says in discussing what it means to produce:

> To create goods is of course not to bring into being materials that never existed before, and it is therefore not creation in the true sense of the word. It is only a conversion of inde-structible matter into more advantageous forms, and it can never be anything else. (1959, p. 7)

Mankind did not develop its fabulous stock of capital equipment by acquiring new quantities of iron and wood and copper and silicon. These have always been here. Mankind became wealthy by developing the knowledge of what might be done with these substances and building that knowledge into them. The value of our tools is not in their physical substance, however finely alloyed or refined. It is in the quality and quantity of knowledge imprinted on them. As Carl Menger says in his *Principles:*

> Increasing understanding of the causal connections between things and human welfare, and increasing control of the less proximate conditions responsible for human welfare, have led mankind, therefore, from a state of barbarism and the deepest

misery to its present stage of civilization and well-being. . . .
Nothing is more certain than that the degree of economic
progress of mankind will still, in future epochs, be commensu-
rate with the degree of progress of human knowledge. (1981,
p. 74. See also Vaughn 1990.)

VARIETIES OF KNOWLEDGE EMBODIED IN CAPITAL

In the above passage Menger asserts a dependency of economic
progress on progress of human knowledge. This sounds simple.
Perhaps it would be simple if knowledge were a simple, homogeneous something which could be pumped into a society as fuel is
pumped into a tank. But knowledge is heterogeneous; it is not all
of a kind (Polanyi 1958, Hayek 1945, Lachmann 1986). There are
important differences among different kinds of knowledge that
have to be taken into account if we are to understand how that
knowledge gets embodied in capital goods.

Articulate and Tacit Knowledge

An important distinction in this respect is between articulate and
inarticulate, or tacit, knowledge.[5] Some of our knowledge we can
articulate: we can say precisely what we know, and thereby convey
it to others.[6] But much of our knowledge is tacit: we cannot say
with any kind of precision what we know or how we know it.
Hence we cannot explicitly convey that knowledge to others, at
least not in words. The experienced personnel officer cannot tell
us how she knows that a certain applicant is unfit for a certain job;
she has "a feel for it." The skilled pianist cannot tell us how to play
with deep expressiveness, although he clearly knows how. A child
cannot learn to hit a baseball from reading about it in a book,
although the book might help. A skilled object-oriented software
designer has a knack for "finding the objects" that will make an
application robust and evolvable, but cannot simply tell others
what she does and how.

---

5 For a full discussion of tacit knowledge, see Michael Polanyi's *The Tacit Dimension.*

6 Those others, of course, bringing to our words different experience and outlook, will
   understand what we say somewhat differently than we do.

Furthermore, much of what we know we are not aware that we know! In such cases we do not become consciously aware of our knowledge until it is somehow brought to our attention, perhaps by our being asked to behave in a way that conflicts with that knowledge. "Let's do such and such," we are asked. "No, that won't work," we reply. "Why not?" "Well, it won't . . .," we say, but we can't really say why until we take time to think about it, and become explicitly aware, for the first time, of what we have long known. In this respect I remember my high school physics teacher telling our class that we all "knew" the Doppler effect—that the sound made by a moving object seems higher pitched to us when the object is approaching, and seems lower pitched when the object is moving away. He smiled and made the sound every child makes when imitating a fast car or airplane going past. Sure enough, the pitch goes from higher to lower. Of course I knew that, but I had not known that I knew it.

The case is similar with much of the knowledge that goes into software. Certain basic ways of doing business are second nature to people in a particular company, so much so that they are not consciously aware of them and thus cannot describe them at, for example, the "requirements stage" of a software development project. As we shall see, this lack of conscious awareness of much of what people know has important implications for how software developers should try to incorporate this kind of knowledge into new software.

Personal and Intersubjective Knowledge

There is also an important variety in what we may call imprecisely the locations of knowledge. Knowledge may, of course, be internal, located within a person. It may also be external, however, embodied in some *intersubjective* medium. That is, it may be located, as it were, *among* people, and therefore available for common use. In each of these locations there may be both articulate and inarticulate knowledge. I know my own verbalizable thoughts and plans for the day, facts I learned in school, my phone number, and so on. This is articulate knowledge in my own mind. Articulate knowledge can also be located externally, intersubjectively, in a form in which it can be transferred among people. This is the case with books, libraries, manuals, "for sale" signs, and so on.

As we have seen, internal personal knowledge may also be inarticulate. Most of our physical skills are of this kind. Our habits seem to represent a kind of inarticulate knowledge (in our habitual looking both ways before we cross streets is the knowledge that streets are dangerous), as do rules of thumb ("honesty is the best policy," "get it in writing"), and social mores ("wait your turn").

Some extremely important kinds of knowledge (unfortunately, though understandably, less appreciated than other kinds) are both inarticulate and external to individuals. Social institutions embody this kind of knowledge. Language, for example, embodies a vast wealth of shared knowledge, accumulated over ages through interactions among people. As F. A. Hayek has stressed, there is more knowledge in market prices than anyone can begin to comprehend.[7] Don Lavoie has developed this view (1985, Chapter 3), speaking of a "social intelligence" that emerges out of the interactions of people, which the society as a whole has, but no individual has.

In this category of inarticulate external knowledge available to be shared among individuals is much of the knowledge embodied in tools. The crucial knowledge referred to by Menger is of a kind we don't often think of as knowledge. It is not to be found in libraries or in books or in written words. Rather it is to be found in the designs of the tools we use. Much of it is inarticulate. Some of it may once have been articulated, but the articulation is now lost. Much may never have been articulated at all. Consider, for example, the ratio between the weight of a hammer head and the length of the handle. Hammer makers "know" the acceptable bounds of this ratio. How do they know? They know because the experience of generations has been handed down to them. Users of hammers, ages ago, found hammers with handles too long or too

---

7 See Hayek's celebrated article, "The Use of Knowledge in Society" (1945). He points out that because prices emerge from the to-buy-or-not-to-buy decisions of all the people "in the market" for that kind of good, they reflect everyone's knowledge of the uses that can be made of that good, various different supplies of it, possible substitutes for it, and so on.

short to be uncomfortable; they discarded these and used the proper-sized ones instead. They could not have said why they did so—they knew with their hands and arms, not with their heads. When they selected new hammers, they chose the ones with the "correct" ratio. From these choices hammer makers learned what the correct ratio was. The knowledge was gradually built into hammers over time, in an evolutionary fashion that depended on feedback from users (Salin 1990).

A significant proportion of the knowledge we use in production is not in any person or group, but in the tools we use. I who use the hammer know nothing of ergonomics, and have not the slightest idea what the correct ratio of head weight to handle length is. Nevertheless, when I drive a nail, I can tell if the hammer feels right. Thus I use that knowledge. The knowledge is built into my hammer.

CAPITAL GOODS AND DIVISION OF KNOWLEDGE ACROSS TIME AND SPACE

There is a distinctly social nature to capital goods and to the capital structure which they compose. Most individual capital goods are manifestations of a far-flung division of knowledge, an extensive sharing of many specialists' knowledge and talent across time and space. The ever-changing pattern of the interactions of these capital goods—the capital structure as a whole—is beyond our grasp. It is a part of what Hayek called "the extended order of human cooperation." To pursue further this idea that capital goods and the capital structure manifest a profound social interaction, let us consider Adam Smith's discussion of the division of labor, to which he attributed the lion's share of human progress.

Recall Smith's case of improvement to the steam engine, which grew out of a small boy's observation that he could tie a piece of string from the handle he was assigned to operate to another part of the machine, and so get the action of the machine to do his job for him. Subsequently, this insight was built into the design of steam engines. When, in cases such as this, knowledge is built into a piece of capital equipment so thoroughly that an actual person is no longer required, what has happened to the division of labor? Has it decreased? The little boy is no longer at work at the steam engine. Does his departure diminish the division of labor present in that production process? There are fewer people on the spot, of course, but on the broad view, are there really fewer contributing?

Or take computer programming. In the earliest days of machines such as ENIAC, the programmers were the people who physically set switches and connected cables, according to the directions of "the program," which had been written on paper by someone else. Now we have compilers to direct the setting of the machine's transistors for us. Are there really fewer people involved, then, when one of us writes and executes a program with a modern computer?

It appears that what Adam Smith meant by the division of labor was the division, among a number of different people, of all the tasks in a particular production process. Given a number of tasks which are visibly part of the production process, the fewer the instances in which the same person carries out more than one of those tasks, the greater the division of labor. This view is evident in Smith's remarks on agriculture:

> The nature of agriculture, indeed, does not admit of so many subdivisions of labour, nor of so complete a separation of one business from another, as manufactures. It is impossible to separate so entirely, the business of the grazier from that of the corn-farmer, as the trade of the carpenter is commonly separated from that of the smith. The spinner is almost always a distinct person from the weaver; but the ploughman, the harrower, the sower of the seed, and the reaper of the corn, are often the same (1976, pp. 9–10).

Here Smith focuses on division of labor among those directly involved in a production process: how many laborers are involved *at that time and place,* given the tools they have. We take issue with Smith, holding that the division of labor is better understood as the whole pattern of cooperation in production, direct and indirect. The indirect contributions are, in an advanced economy, the most significant. As Carl Menger pointed out, the crucial "labor" is the creative effort of learning how[8] and embodying that learning in a tool design that can be used by others, who themselves lack the knowledge in any other form. We really do better to speak of the division of knowledge rather than the division of labor.

Axel Leijonhufvud makes clear the importance of the division of knowledge in his article, "Information Costs and the Division of Labor" (1989). He invites us to consider a medieval serf named Bodo and asks "Why was he poor?" Leijonhufvud argues, "Bodo was poor because few people co-operated with him in producing his output and, similarly, few people co-operated in producing his real income, i.e. in producing for his consumption" (p. 166). The cooperation need not be on the same spot and at the same time to be relevant. Indeed, as an economy advances, the pattern of cooperation spreads out spatially and in time.

> Our rich twentieth-century representative man, then, occupies a node in a much larger network of co-operating individual agents than did poor Bodo. His network, moreover, is of very much larger spatial extent. The average distance from him of those who contribute to his consumption or make use of his productive contribution is longer. Similarly, his network also has greater temporal depth—the number of individuals who t periods into the past made a contribution to his present consumption is larger than in Bodo's case (Leijonhufvud 1989, p. 166).

In his comments on the division of labor in agriculture, Smith neglects the division of knowledge and of labor embodied in the tools the farmers use. The plough, the harrow, and the scythe—or, in our day, the laser plane—themselves represent an extensive division of labor and, more importantly, of knowledge. Smith's classic example of the division of labor, from the very first chapter of the *Wealth of Nations*, concerned a pin factory in which ten different workmen, each specializing on a different job, could together make many times more pins than they could make if they were to work individually, each doing every task himself. To be consistent with

---

[8] (Menger 1981). For a discussion of Menger's criticism, see Vaughn (1990).

his suggestion in the quoted passage on agriculture, Smith would have to assert that there is less division of labor represented in the present-day manufacture of pins, in which (if I guess correctly) hundreds of thousands may be made in a day in a fully mechanized process overseen by one technician at a computer terminal, than in the small factory of which he wrote.

But the fact that there is now only one person there on the spot does not mean there is no division of labor in modern pin making. It illustrates, rather, that the division of labor is now more subtle. It is manifested not in many workers, but in sophisticated tools to which many creative workers have contributed their special knowledge of the steps (what used to be the tasks) involved in pin making. Today's equivalent of Smith's division of labor is manifested in a complex division of knowledge embedded in a deep pin-making capital structure.

As Thomas Sowell has observed, "[T]he intellectual advantage of civilization . . . is not necessarily that each civilized man has more knowledge [than primitive savages], but that he *requires* far *less*" (1980, p. 7, emphasis in original). Through the embodiment of knowledge into an extending capital structure, each of us is able to take advantage of the specialized knowledge of untold others who have contributed to that structure. The structure becomes increasingly complex over time, as the pattern of complementary relationships extends.[9]

In capital-intensive, modern production processes, the division of knowledge and labor is to be found not in the large number of people at work in a particular production process, but in the tools used by a very few people who carry out that process. The knowledge contribution of multitudes is embodied in those tools, which give remarkable productive powers to the individual workers on the spot. The little boy is there in a modern steam engine, his knowledge embodied in the valve-control rod. The farmer at his plough is empowered by the knowledge and labor of hundreds of

---

[9] Lachmann credits Hayek (1935) with "reinterpreting the extended time dimension of capital as an increasing degree of complexity of the pattern of complementarity displayed by the capital structure" (1975, p. 4).

others, who designed his plough and hardened its steel, who developed his tractor, who learned how to refine its fuel, and so on. The programmer using a modern object-oriented development environment is empowered by the knowledge and labor of those who built the user interface, compiler, the browsing tools, the classes in the class hierarchy, and so on.

The point is emphasized by Bohm-Bawerk, who in the following passage could be responding to Smith's above comments on agriculture.

> . . . the labor which produces the intermediate products . . . and the labor which produces the desired consumption good from and with the help of the intermediate products, contribute alike to the production of that consumption good. The obtaining of wood results not only from the labor of felling trees, but also from that of the smith who makes the axe, of the carpenter who carves the haft, of the miner who digs the ore from which the steel is derived, of the foundryman who smelts the ore. Our modern system of specialized occupations does, of course, give the intrinsically unified process of production the extrinsic appearance of a heterogeneous mass of apparently independent units. But the theorist who makes any pretensions to understanding the economic workings of the production process in all its vital relationships must not be deceived by appearances, his mind must restore the unity of the production process which has had its true picture obscured by the division of labor. (1959, II, p. 85)

What a difference there is between the meaning Bohm-Bawerk attaches to the division of labor in this passage and the view suggested by Adam Smith in his comments on agriculture. For Bohm-Bawerk and for us, the division of labor is extended down time and across space. The miner of the ore is "there," in a sense, as the lumberjack fells trees with steel made from that ore. In an advancing economy, the division of knowledge is an ever-widening system of cooperation in which are developed new tools and processes whereby each person may take advantage of the knowledge of an increasing number of his or her fellows. The division of knowledge is manifested in the tools we work with, which embody the knowledge of many.

CAPITAL STRUCTURE

Capital exists and works within a structure (Lachmann 1978, Hayek 1941). It is an ever-evolving structure to be sure—it is never static—but at any time the relationships among capital goods, and among capital goods and the skills of the people who use them (sometimes called human capital), are essential. Of the various perspectives we might take on capital structure, three will be especially important to us. One focuses on the relationships of complementarity between capital goods used jointly in a production process; another focuses on relationships of dependency between capital goods, one or more of which are used in producing another; a third focuses on the categories of capital goods and other knowledge inputs which are involved in production processes.

COMPLEMENTARITY OF THE ESSENCE

The complementarities among different capital goods—their interdependencies and synergies, the ways they enable, augment, or extend one another's effectiveness—are crucial. Ludwig Lachmann stresses the point:

> It is hard to imagine any capital resource which by itself, operated by human labour but without the use of other capital resources, could turn out any output at all. For most purposes capital goods have to be used jointly. *Complementarity* is of the essence of capital use. But the heterogeneous capital resources do not lend themselves to combination in any arbitrary fashion. For any given number of them only certain modes of complementarity are technically possible, and only a few of these are economically significant. (1978, p. 3, emphasis in original)

Programming languages run only on certain kinds of computers. A complex programming environment such as Smalltalk requires further that the computer be equipped with a mouse and a high-resolution display. The various graphical user interface builders for Smalltalk run only where certain specific versions of Smalltalk are present. These are very powerful tools, but usable only if the necessary complementary goods are present.

When new capital goods are developed—when capital is accumulated and the capital structure lengthens and becomes more productive—what is generally involved is the development of new, more complex patterns of complementarity. The new capital goods must fit with the old (and other new goods) in order to be useful. The lengthening of the capital structure involves what Lachmann calls a " 'division of capital,' a specialization of individual capital items" (1978, p. 79). We might call it a "complexifying" of the capital structure, an increasing intricacy of the pattern(s) of complementarity among increasingly specialized capital goods, born in the ongoing growth and division of knowledge.[10] Developers of new capital goods must be very attentive to the fit of their new designs with others extant or in development.

We will devote a whole chapter, Chapter 4, to the subject of capital maintenance, focusing on software maintenance. In the present context it is important to point out that the challenge of capital maintenance has to do fundamentally with complementarity. Capital exists and functions in a structure in which complementarities are fundamentally important, and the capital structure evolves over time as old tools and processes are supplanted by new. Consequently, for any particular (kind of) capital good, maintenance is a matter of maintaining its complementarity to the rest of the changing capital structure. Hence maintenance may mean not only preventing any change through deterioration, but actually changing that (kind of) good directly, in a manner that adapts it to the changing capital structure around it, and thereby delaying obsolescence or increasing usefulness.

Because change is pervasive, how a particular (kind of) capital good is used will inevitably change. As Hayek (1935) has pointed out, capital maintenance is often more a matter of maintaining the *value* of capital than merely preventing decay. But because value

---

[10]Lachmann, following Hayek (1935), holds that over time there develops "an increasing degree of complexity of the pattern of complementarity displayed by the capital structure" (1975, p. 4).

depends on position in a changing capital structure, maintaining value may mean *changing* the good more than preserving it as is.

Software, of course, does not deteriorate. (A diskette may, but a diskette is software's storage medium, not software itself.) Yet programmers speak of "bit rot," that creeping incompatibility that erodes software's usefulness as the environment changes—new computers, peripherals, operating systems, down-sizing to client-server systems—but the code does not. Bit rot is purely a matter of complementarity. Maintaining the value of a piece of software, even when what it does stays exactly the same, requires changing that software to keep it complementary to the changing capital goods with which it must work.

ORDERS OF CAPITAL GOODS

A useful way in which to think of the capital structure is in terms of what economists call *orders of goods.* In this way of thinking, consumer goods are called goods *of the first order,* and the capital goods that serve in producing them are goods of ever-higher orders as they are involved in processes increasingly distant from the final consumer good. As the capital structure lengthens, we develop tools for producing tools for producing tools. Every step up the chain is a step to a higher order. Milk, for example, is a good of the first order. We might treat the cow and the hay she eats as goods of the second order, the field in which the hay is produced as a good of the third order, the laser plane that leveled the field as a good of the fourth order, and so on. There is nothing really significant about the particular numbers; what is useful is the concept of higher- and lower-order goods. With this concept we can easily think and speak of lengthening chains of production in the capital structure, as more and more goods of higher order are incorporated into an ever-more-complex structure of production.

The better the tools at each stage, the better and more cheaply we may produce the goods at the next lower stage. Menger stressed the importance of lengthening the capital structure:

> Assume a people which extends its attention to goods of third, fourth, and higher orders. . . . If such a people progressively directs goods of ever higher orders to the satisfaction of its

needs, and especially if each step in this direction is accompanied by an appropriate division of labor, we shall doubtless observe that progress in welfare which Adam Smith was disposed to attribute exclusively to the latter factor. (p. 73)

Improvements in tools (and related processes) of high order are very important to economic development, because those improvements can be leveraged throughout the production process.

Frequently, there is a kind of recursion involved, in that developments at one stage make possible developments at another stage, which can in turn improve processes at the first stage. Better steel, for example—the product of a steel mill—makes possible the construction of still better steel mills. The availability of Smalltalk made possible the user interface builder WindowBuilder, which is itself an improvement to Smalltalk.

In most of what follows we will be concerned with goods of fairly high order; in particular, we will be concerned with tools for the design of (software) tools. To clarify this point, we need to consider briefly the different categories of capital inputs to a production process.

CATEGORIES OF CAPITAL GOODS

What are the categories of capital goods at work in production processes? In common parlance there are two; the first is known as *fixed capital,* "producer durables," or, more generally, tools. The second is known as *working capital,* raw materials or intermediate goods, or goods in process. Examples come readily to mind when we envision a production process. In a steel mill, the mill machinery is the fixed capital, the iron ingots and molten metal are the working capital. In a bakery, the baker's oven and rolling pin are the fixed capital, the flour and dough are the working capital. In a business context, the word processors, spreadsheet programs, and database managers are fixed capital, and a company's texts and financial data are working capital, to be processed by the spreadsheet into, say, a meaningful report.

For programmers using early programming languages to produce software, only fixed capital, in the form of the programming language and its compiler, were available. There were no raw materials or intermediate goods to work with: the programmer started with a blank screen. The picture has changed and continues to change for the better, however. Today's programmers have their languages and compilers, but also an increasing range of tools. Perhaps more significantly, they often have working capital in the form of pre-defined classes, design patterns, and other components which they can use directly or adapt to their purposes.

Capital does not work by itself, of course. In order to be productive, it must be put in motion and directed by people according to some plan, in a set of procedures. Hence procedures are an essential complement to capital in production, and should be kept in mind as such when we examine how the capital structure evolves.[11] Fixed capital, working capital, and procedures are inextricably interrelated, because procedures will be couched in terms of what tools do to materials. You can't have procedures without the other two. The procedures themselves can be stored (embodied) in a variety of ways, for example, in written documents; in the "human capital" of a skilled worker's mind, muscles, or senses; in development methodologies, and even in rituals.

An illuminating example of a procedure stored in a non-material fashion is that of the ritual of sword-making in ancient Japan.

> [T]he techniques that produce the special properties of steel ... reach their climax, for me, in the making of the Japanese sword, which has been going on in one way or another since A.D. 800. The making of the sword, like all ancient metallurgy, is surrounded with ritual, and that is for a clear reason. When you have no written language, when you have nothing that can be called a chemical formula, then you must have a precise ceremonial which fixes the sequence of operations so that they are exact and memorable. . . .
>
> The temperature of the steel for this final moment [when it is plunged into water to cool] has to be judged precisely, and in a civilisation in which that is not done by measurement, "it

---

[11] I am tempted to call procedures a *kind* of capital, except that to do so would depart too much from common usage.

is the practice to watch the sword being heated until it glows to the colour of the morning sun." (Bronowski 1973, pp. 131–33)

As technology progresses, routines are frequently built into capital goods, and thereby become part of the capital itself. For example, a grain combine embodies in that one machine the harvesting routine of first cutting, then threshing, then separating the grain from the chaff. It is frequently the task of computer programs to embody production procedures. Whereas in old-fashioned sword making, for example, the routine was separate from the tools it directed—"stored" in the ritual passed on from person to person—in modern sword making, the routines are *embodied* in the software and sensors of the machinery used. When the sensors says the metal is the right temperature, the software directs the machinery to plunge it into the cooling bath. The routine has been embodied in a tool; it has become part of the capital.

Fixed capital, working capital, and procedures—is that all? No. These three imply some purpose, some end aim. Our procedures for applying tools to raw materials aim at producing *something*. This something must be conceived, more or less fully. To put it another way, it must be *designed* in some degree. Producers must have some implicit or explicit design to inform their actions. This design, this conceptualization or description of what is aimed at, guides the procedures.

In this category fall preliminary sketches, detailed blueprints and specifications, CAD pictures in all their range of possible detail, vague mental pictures, detailed models, software prototypes as well as completed code, and even generally accepted definitions. Examples are the "steel rail," the design of which (probably in the form of a detailed specification) informs the procedures of the steel mill, "loaf of bread," which informs the procedures of the baker, and some notion of a report on profitability projections, which informs the procedures of the business analyst.

Thus we have four elements of production processes: a) tools or fixed capital, b) raw or intermediate material, or working capital, c) procedures for applying the tools to the raw or intermediate goods, and d) designs that inform the procedures.

DESIGNING CAPITAL GOODS AS A SOCIAL LEARNING PROCESS

Consider the implied context of the above discussion. We spoke of production processes—implicitly, of *known* production processes aimed at producing *known* goods. The designs of which we spoke, which inform the procedures that direct fixed capital in processing working capital, are themselves implicitly known. But this begs important questions. Where do the designs come from? How are they produced? What is the process by which they come to be?

It is important here to draw a clear distinction between producing designs for goods and producing individual instances of those goods. The production processes for the two are quite different. And, living as we do in a physical world, where physical instances catch our eye, it is easy to overlook the production of designs and see only the production of instances. Economics, certainly, has overlooked the production of designs, by and large assuming it away. Standard models assume "given technology" or "use of the best available technology." But for our purposes—investigating how the capital structure develops and improves—it is essential to focus on the production of designs as an activity different from the production of particular goods embodying those designs.

Let us clarify the distinction by contrasting our common conceptions of producing cars, on the one hand, and of producing software, on the other. When we think of GM "producing cars," we think of their work creating new instances of extant designs. True, GM employs many designers, who *design* new cars, but we don't think of that. We think of the assembly line, spot welding, riveting, bolting, and so on: the hard work of realizing these designs, the imprinting of the design on metal and rubber and glass so that a new instance of the design—a new car—comes to be.

When we think of Microsoft's work producing software, by contrast, we think of programmers writing code—creating new designs (or enhancing older designs). True, Microsoft employs people who store the programs onto diskettes, thus in a sense creating instances of the extant designs; but we don't think of that. We think of the late nights at the terminal designing, coding, revising, running, debugging, and so on, the hard work of creating new software—new designs—specific instances of which will eventually be copied in mass onto diskettes and distributed.

The point here is not that design is unimportant in heavy industries such as automobile manufacturing.[12] Not at all. In fact, we hold that design is just as important in such industries as in software. Indeed, by way of example, the design process for the GM-10 line of cars at General Motors was allocated $7 billion and five years (Womack *et al.* 1990, pp. 104–6). The point is simply that designing capital goods and what we will call their instantiation— the creation of actual instances of those designs—are fundamentally different kinds of processes. Instantiation is concerned with the known, design with the unknown. Instantiation is a matter of imprinting a design onto a medium; design is a matter of bringing together and articulating in symbols the knowledge of how to accomplish some productive purpose.

Because design is a process of bringing together and embodying productive knowledge in a handy, ready-to-use form, design is a learning process. Because that knowledge is of different kinds and widely dispersed among different people and institutions, design is a social learning process—it depends on the interaction of a number of people. Capital is embodied knowledge. *The designing of capital, the developing of the capital structure, is a social learning process whereby knowledge is embodied in usable form.*

What is the nature of this process? What makes it go forward in a better or worse manner? We turn now to an examination of software development, in order to find some answers to these questions.

---

[12]Indeed, product design in manufacturing industries is receiving a lot of attention. See Wheelwright and Clark (1992), and Womack *et al.* (1990).

A Short History of
Software Development

*Yet I doubt not through the ages one increasing purpose runs,
And the thoughts of men are widened with the process of the suns.*

—Tennyson, "Locksley Hall"

*. . . it's taken us years to understand just how hard it is to build
good software. Developing robust, large-scale software systems
that can evolve to meet changing needs turns out to be one of the
most demanding challenges in modern technology.*

—David Taylor (1990, p. 2)

INTRODUCTION

At this point, we devote a short chapter to a brief historical
overview of software development processes and tools, and how
they have evolved. The chapter is essentially an interpretation of
the evolution of programming practice from the perspective of an
Austrian school economist who is interested in capital theory.

We first consider the main forces that have driven the evolution of programming practice. Foremost among these is the astonishing fall in prices of computer processing power and memory,
which has enabled ever-larger and more ambitious programming
projects. With more ambitious projects come greater learning
challenges. The main challenge, which we take up next, has been
maintaining coordination in a complex learning process distributed across many interacting people and modules. Doing so is difficult, and a variety of tools and development methodologies have
been put into practice to try to meet this challenge; we take an

overview of these. We finish by introducing object-oriented programming systems (OOPS) and related technologies, a relative newcomer to the field that seems to hold real promise for enabling coordination in these complex capital structures.

OVERVIEW: FROM RESOURCE CONSTRAINT TO COMPLEXITY CONSTRAINT

As colleagues and I have pointed out elsewhere (Lavoie, Baetjer, and Tulloh 1991, 1992), the evolution of programming practice seems to have been driven by the steady drop in the price of computational resources. As processing power, memory, and storage space have dropped dramatically in price, people's software ambitions have grown apace. At one time programming was mainly *resource-constrained:* with processing power and memory scarce and expensive, our programs were necessarily simple, and programmers concentrated on making the most of scarce machine resources. After all, if a program was too big, it would not fit into the computer; if it was not very cleverly executed, it would take prohibitively long to run. Given these limits, the amount of knowledge (speaking imprecisely) we tried to embody in programs was small, and therefore the learning process involved was comparatively simple.

The resource constraint has been steadily and dramatically relaxed by the prodigious accomplishments of hardware manufacturers. As a result, the programs we try to build have become more and more ambitious and complex. We can afford—in respect to memory requirements—to build big programs because memory is cheap. We can afford—in respect to processing power—to demand a tremendous amount of computation because our machines are so fast. In short, we can afford—in respect to physical resources generally—very big, very complex programs. Of course, we do try to build such programs. But these ambitious projects attempt to embody a large amount of different knowledge, from various different sources, with multiple complex dependencies among the parts. Accordingly, the learning process involved in building these programs is comparatively more complex.

Team programming One source of increased complexity arises from the very division of knowledge on which major software projects depend. As the software industry has grown in size and ambition, software development has of necessity become less and less a solitary activity, and more and more a group endeavor, with many people contributing their knowledge and talent to the development of a particular system. This is team programming—division of labor in software development. It is not unusual to have scores of programmers all working on the same project. The different programmers are often separated both geographically and temporally, as they work on different parts of a large system in different locales and on different schedules.

Integration of functions Another source of greater complexity is the integration of various functions into one software system. There was a time when each application stood more or less alone. Now, however, we want our different software tools to "talk to" one another—we want them to *complement* one another. A simple example is the integration of word-processing, spreadsheet, and graphics capabilities: modern word processors import drawings, charts, and tabular data from other programs. A different kind of integration is the "embedding" of software into physical machines. "Embedded systems" direct machines, for example, sensing and controlling movements of robot arms, temperatures in ovens, and the flow of inventory through a manufacturing process.

Networking Still another source of complexity is networking. Programs were once confined to the computer that they ran on. Now, with improved telecommunications and computer networking, computation has become very much a social process. It is increasingly imprecise to say that certain programs run "on a computer." Frequently, they run on several machines at once, their functionality extended across the network, with many people interacting through them; such applications are known as *distributed applications*. For example, automated teller systems interlink a host of different automated teller machines at many different sites, serving many different banks. In the new world of distributed applications, it is said, with increasing accuracy, that "the network is the computer."

All this increased complexity threatens to discoordinate and disintegrate the learning process. In short, as we have made great progress in overcoming the resource constraint on programming, we have a encountered a *complexity constraint*. A successful new tool (whether software or hardware) is one in which all the requisite knowledge is effectively integrated. As the tool becomes more complex, embodying more and more interdependent knowledge, the learning process by which all that knowledge must be successfully integrated becomes more and more challenging.

THE KEY CHALLENGE: COORDINATING DISTRIBUTED LEARNING

The primary constraint on programming today is not physical resources, but the very complexity of what we are trying to do, and the limits of our ability to manage that complexity. As Mark S. Miller of Agorics, Inc. puts it, the key limitation is "our sheer ability to understand what it is we are trying to do."[1]

As programs grow in magnitude and complexity, division of knowledge becomes a necessity. There is a limit to how much code one person can keep in mind and work with at one time, so the task must be split up somehow. Merely to get a grasp on what is happening, we have to abstract from the whole problem, *decomposing* it somehow into subsystems and subproblems (of succeeding levels) that different people may work on, or the same person at different times. This decomposition occurs in various ways, some of which we will examine below. But one way or another, large programs must be split up into different modules, in order to allow the programmers to focus on the different parts of the problem. "This general strategy is known as *modular programming,* and it forms the guiding principle behind most of the advances in software construction in the past forty years" (Taylor 1990, p. 3).

---

[1] Personal conversation.

Modular programming, then, is a manifestation of division of knowledge in capital. In modules, different sets of knowledge are embodied in such a way that they can usefully be shared across time and space. But of course, merely to divide knowledge into modules does not ensure success. The modules must be *complementary* to one another in use. That means both that they must fit, and also that people who use them must be able to see without too much trouble just *how* they fit. How the abstraction boundaries are drawn is important. Appropriate abstractions provide orderly interaction and understandability; inappropriate abstractions cause problems.

A major problem programmers face is maintaining complementarity among modules. Even when only one person is working on a complex problem, it is easy to forget, or simply to misunderstand, the effect that one module may have on another, and thus to build in unwanted (side) effects—bugs. Much of debugging a program has been to this point a matter of ironing out all these unintended interferences of one module with another. As we will see, better-conceived ways of drawing abstraction boundaries can significantly diminish this discoordination.

Of course, large projects are often undertaken by large groups of people, with a different person or team working on each module, and with a system architect or system designer overseeing development at a high level. With this division of knowledge not only among different modules but also among people, there arise additional problems of maintaining complementarity among the modules of the evolving software. These have been explicated well by Fred Brooks in his celebrated book, *The Mythical Man-Month* (1975). Brooks emphasizes the importance of communication. The different team members must keep informed of what assumptions being made by others, which will affect what they themselves are working on. There can be great difficulty in maintaining effective communication and clear understandings among the members of a team when the team grows large. At some point the sheer cost of maintaining effective communication exceeds the value of the additional brain power.

THE EVOLUTION OF PROGRAMMERS' CAPITAL GOODS

In response to the challenge of managing the ever-increasing complexity of software, the software industry is constantly evolving higher-order capital goods and corresponding processes to help developers build knowledge into software in an orderly, effective way. These tools for designing software tools, including new programming languages and a variety of tools and processes, can be understood as aids to the social learning process. Sometimes they simply automate processes, freeing the programmer from having to know how to do something at all. This is the case with compilers, which handle the detail of putting code into machine language, and code generators, which can generate code according to some other (usually graphical) representation. Development methodologies aim (some accurately, some inaccurately) at organizing the social learning process so that it can proceed smoothly. Many of the programmers' tools as such contribute directly to programmers' understanding of what they are doing.

PROGRAMMING LANGUAGES

Of course, a primary aid to managing complexity is the development of better programming languages. These languages themselves embody an increasing amount of others' knowledge of how to program. Each new generation of languages has given programmers more power to express complex relationships by capturing and expressing higher-level abstractions. Each has given programmers more freedom from the concerns of the computer itself—such minutia as what value is in what register—because the knowledge of how to handle that minutia is embodied in the language's compiler. Accordingly, programmers using these higher-level languages are enabled to think more in terms of the problem they are trying to solve and less in terms of how the computer operates to solve it.

The evolution of programming languages gives us a classic instance of the way better tools enable a division of knowledge across time and space. In the earliest days, on machines such as ENIAC, the "programmers" were relatively unskilled clerks who actually twisted dials and moved connector cables on the machine. In place of this physical manipulation there is now machine language; with the advent of machine language people were freed from the necessity to set switches and connections physically. Up a level of abstraction from this is assembly language, still highly numerical and concerned with the needs of the machine. Then came higher-level languages with compilers which translated their code into machine language. Gradually, as one passes to higher- and higher-level languages, the code becomes less oriented to the characteristics and needs of the machine and more attuned to humans' characteristics and thought processes. Accordingly, programmers using these languages can think more in terms of symbols or even familiar words which represent aspects of the problem domain they are trying to represent, unconcerned with the details of how a particular machine will store and manipulate bits and bytes. Because others have figured out how to manage the bits and bytes, and embodied that knowledge in the compiler, it is no longer necessary for programmers to have that knowledge themselves.

At the same time higher-level languages provide better abstraction capability, they provide more discipline—and, hence, understandability and coherence—to the code. In other words, they embody knowledge of what *not* to do. Somewhat paradoxically, languages which provide programmers great freedom thereby provide them rope with which to hang themselves. Programmers using some of the early languages soon learned to write subroutines— sequences of instructions treated as separate units, which can be called from anywhere in a program—to which they directed program flow with GOTO statements. But the unrestricted use of GOTO statements leads to "spaghetti code," in which the relationships among different modules are difficult or impossible to perceive, making life difficult for anyone, including the original programmer, who might come back to work on this code.

Structured programming languages address this problem by providing programmers a relatively small but comprehensive set of functions for directing program flow, so that the underlying structure of the program is much clearer and more understandable. Despite this advance, structured programming languages still have the problem that their programs share a common pool of data. Although the functions that the program performs are separated into clearly-structured, separate routines, all the data that the program uses is centralized and accessible to any of those routines. As a consequence, too frequently one routine may change data structures in a manner not anticipated by other routines, leading to nonsense—bugs.

A recent response to this difficulty (and others) is object-oriented languages. Because these seem to constitute such an important advance, we will take them up in some detail in the last section of this chapter.

DEVELOPMENT METHODOLOGIES

Various software development methodologies have evolved along with programming languages. A methodology is a set of procedures that a software development organization follows (or tries to follow) in producing new software. A development methodology can be seen as a kind of template for the social learning process of software development. Again, in the early days, when computers were very limited and problems were relatively simple, no extensive methodology was necessary because the demands on learning were so light. Smart programmers could "hack" a solution, working at the problem in an unstructured way until they solved it. But, as programs grew, this approach broke down. It became impossible to predict when a program would be ready for use, whether or not it would work properly, and, if it did work, whether or not it would be what the customer actually needed.

There grew up in response a move to discipline the software development process, to make it more like other kinds of engineering in being based on sound, established principles and industry-standard processes. Hence the term *software engineering*. Whether because of the youth of the industry, or because of the special difficulties of software, industry-standard processes, with resultant standardization and predictability, have decidedly not emerged. The whole field of software development methodology remains in ferment, with new methodologies growing up amid high hopes, and then fading in disappointment. There has been a coevolution of software development tools to support the various methodologies, and because the technologies, needs, and tools of the industry are changing so rapidly, there is little stability or accepted wisdom. Software development is difficult. As Fred Brooks wrote in the title of a celebrated essay on the subject, there may be "No Silver Bullet" (1987) with which to slay the problems and make software development easy.

Nevertheless, attempts must be made. Traditional methodologies generally consist of some variant of the "waterfall model," in which development cascades from users' requirements to analysis to design to coding to testing to debugging to delivery. Such methodologies are a reaction to the unstructured, experimental approach of the early days. Often they are associated with special tools called CASE tools, CASE standing for *computer-assisted software engineering*. These approaches are sometimes known as *CASE methodologies*. In an attempt to bring the rigor of engineering to software development, these methodologies aim to make clear at the outset exactly what the user wants; this is the *requirements* stage. There follows an *analysis* of the problem domain and the physical environment (that is, computer types and network needs) in which the software will run. Then there is a high-level *design* of the system. The analysis and design are frequently captured in complicated drawings of data flows and entity relationships. Next the *coding* is done; frequently this is a matter of translating the elaborate design drawings into code. Then the code is *tested* and *debugged* and finally, one hopes, delivered to a satisfied customer.

As we will see, these traditional methodologies have fallen short of what was promised from them, often because they assume that requirements can be clearly established at the outset of the development process. Because the knowledge that must be built into software is dispersed and tacit, it is rare to get a clear, complete statement of requirements, especially for a project of any magnitude and complexity. In the early days of electronic computation, computers were used mostly to automate well-known, established processes. Hence the task of the software was reasonably clear. But as programmers became more sophisticated and as people gained experience in using computers, they began to try to take advantage of computers in new ways, not just doing the same old thing faster and cheaper, but doing something new, different, and better. Requirements for such systems cannot be stated clearly at the outset, because people do not know yet what they want. Only as they gain experience with a developing design do they discover what they want and become able to define the requirements.

Many methodologies, and many more software projects, have foundered on the fact that requirements cannot be fully known at the outset. With painful regularity, traditional methodologies have produced, at the cost of hundreds of thousands of dollars and many human-years of effort, fully functional, complete systems that are unusable because they do not do what the customer wants them to do.

Another difficulty with traditional methodologies is the loss of meaning and understanding that frequently occurs in the translation from analysis to design and from design to implementation. Often three different representations are involved: two different kinds of drawings for analysis and design, and code for the implementation. The challenge of maintaining consistency and understandability between them is called *bridging the semantic gap;* frequently, the gap is not successfully bridged. When it is not, the learning process breaks down, and the knowledge that needs to be embodied in the software is lost instead.

Still another problem with traditional methodologies is that they fail to provide for capital structure evolution. They aim to complete the product correctly, when there is no such thing as completion in a world of change. In software terms, these methodologies have failed to take adequate account of the inevitability of maintenance, of maintaining complementarity with other tools around them in a constantly evolving capital structure. There appears to have been, in earlier days, a naive, unexamined belief on the part of many that a software system could be finished, made right, fully suited to the users' purposes. Once this was done, it was thought, the job was finished. Gradually, software developers have become aware that no system is ever finished, unless it is no longer being used. Many have found, to their dismay, that up to 80 percent of their software development costs come in fixing and adapting their product after delivery. Developers are always aiming at a moving target, because users' purposes and the computational environment are always changing. (A fundamental element of this change, which still seems to be poorly understood, is that in using the system, people learn better what can be done and what they would like; *ipso facto* their purposes change.) Change is inherent in the software world (as it is in the rest of the world, of course).

New methodologies are being developed that come to grips with the lack of clear requirements, the tacit, dispersed nature of knowledge, the importance of semantic consistency among analysis, design, and implementation, and the inevitability of maintenance. The most promising of these take advantage of object-oriented technologies, which we discuss below. These approaches generally involve some form of prototyping in the early stages. Prototypes are used as a vehicle through which the designers and users of the new software can come to understand their respective capabilities and needs, thereby establishing system requirements. Because object-oriented programming environments are flexible and pre-supplied with components that can be tailored to new purposes, they enable *rapid prototyping,* in which a prototype can be quickly evolved through several iterations in a kind of dialogue between designers and users. This dialogue is a crucial part of the learning process.

Object-oriented technologies also help to bridge the semantic gap, in that the entire development process, from analysis through coding, can use the same terminology. Those who will use the system, as well as the designers and the programmers who do the nitty-gritty implementation, may think about the problem being addressed in terms of the elements of the system and their interactions: these are represented in the evolving software as *objects* and their *methods.* Instead of having to translate from design diagrams in one notation to code in another, object-oriented programmers doing detailed implementation "simply" fill in the details of the interactions of the objects developed in analysis and design. A related advantage of using the same kind of notation throughout is that analysis, design, and implementation can all be occurring simultaneously (as is often necessary as requirements evolve).

Object-oriented techniques also greatly improve the maintainability of software systems, because their modular structure is understandable, and because it allows changes to be localized. Object-oriented systems generally avoid the problems of "spaghetti code" in which one small change made here necessitates corresponding changes all over the system.

TOOLS

It is difficult to discuss methodologies without considering development tools at the same time, because the two are highly complementary, and often designed to be so. There has been extensive evolution of programmers' tools, aimed at helping with virtually all aspects of software development. Among these are, of course, programming languages, which we have mentioned. There are increasing numbers of programming environments that provide a suite of tools in addition to the language proper. Some of these tools include

- *Debuggers*   These help programmers find and fix mistakes on the screen. (In the early days, one had to get a printout of the program and look through the code by hand to find the error.) These tools are wonderful aids to learning. They help programmers learn what they have actually created and how it actually works, as opposed to what they intended.

- *Compilers*   These translate the more abstract code written in higher-level languages into machine code (binary or executable code) that the computer can run. Good compilers are remarkable in their ability to make trade-offs leading to efficient use of machine resources. As we have said, they embody others' knowledge of the nitty-gritty concerns of the computers, shielding programmers writing applications from these.

- *Diagramming tools*   These are an important kind of CASE tool. They automate the process of drawing the extensive diagrams often used in traditional analysis and design. While they are not much faster than drawing by hand initially, they have the advantage of speeding up (the inevitable) changes considerably. Their main role as aids to learning is that they provide their users a perspective on the program different from that given by the code itself.

- *Code generators*   These translate from a higher-level specification of some kind (for example, certain highly structured kinds of design diagrams or screen layouts) to code. They are especially useful for creating the code necessary for creating user interfaces and reports. More capable and accurate code generators are a much sought after, and elusive, goal of CASE.

- *Version-control tools*   These have been developed in response to the challenge of coordinating the work of large teams of programmers. They help maintain the division of labor and knowledge. They keep track of the different versions of different modules, facilitating team development and helping integrate changes. For example, if module A is used by modules B and C, but then module A must be changed for some reason, a good version-control tool will alert programmers to the dependencies so that they can adjust B and C, if necessary, to restore compatibility.

- *Browsers*   These are relevant primarily to object-oriented languages, which make use of structured hierarchies of abstract data structures called *classes*. Class hierarchy browsers allow programmers to look through the hierarchy easily, browsing for classes that may be useful to them. In general, browsers allow programmers to examine different aspects of programs and systems from a variety of different viewpoints. These different viewpoints give them a better grasp of different aspects of the complex systems they are building.

"AUTOMATIC PROGRAMMING" AND AUGMENTATION OF HUMAN CREATIVITY

To what extent can the process of software development be automated? Computers can do so much, can they produce software? How necessary are people to the software production process? These questions concern the potential of what has been called "automatic programming" and the more general subject of automated support for software engineering. Some have held that software production can be automated, and point to developments which, they claim, prove their case. There is a fair amount of attention given today to automatic code generators, which automatically produce executable code from diagrams or other visual representations of program concepts. Some CASE tool builders provide this kind of capability, at least in limited fashion.

Another school of thought holds that automatic programming is a chimera, that only people write programs, and that the idea of automatic programming is fundamentally mistaken. There is a great deal that computers cannot do in producing software; they can do none of the interesting, hard problems.

These positions, though ostensibly in conflict, are reconcilable when couched in a different way. As we will see in the next chapter, the meaning of automatic programming has evolved in a revealing way. For now it suffices to say that while some kinds of activities can be automated, others appear to be impossible to automate. But unquestionably computer tools can help people in their tasks by *augmenting* human capabilities (Englebart 1963).

The dispute about the potential for automatic programming, and its *de facto* resolution in the nature of the new tools and processes being developed, point up an important aspect of the evolution of programming practice. That is, software engineers are gradually discovering and accepting that software development is an ongoing process and must be treated as such. In general terms familiar to economists, the capital structure is not static; therefore capital goods, to maintain their value—their position of usefulness in the evolving capital structure—must evolve. Because the software industry has learned that change is inevitable, both in the initial development period and after products are put to use, many of the most useful languages, tools, and methodologies now being developed are those that help software developers manage change. Of these, perhaps the most important are the object-oriented technologies. We finish this chapter with a short introduction to these.

OBJECT ORIENTATION AND SOCIAL LEARNING

Object technology has a number of features that support the social learning process. They help people work together by fostering the division of labor; they help people communicate by offering a flexible language in which to do so; and they help everyone involved understand what they are doing.

Object-oriented programming systems have their origins in the programming language Simula, which was designed to enable the construction of computer simulations. The units of interest in Simula are the objects in the system being simulated. What made Simula different from previous languages is that its modules were composed not of functional units only, like traditional subroutines, but of combinations of functions and related data. From this idea, object-oriented technologies were born.

An object, then, is a bundle of related data and functionality. The concept is a simple and natural one, smoothly applicable to modeling natural systems. Consider an airplane, for example. This is an object defined by certain data, including its cruising speed, carrying capacity, age, location, and so on, as well as by the functions that it can carry out, such as taking off, cruising, landing, and taxiing. In the pure object-oriented systems such as Smalltalk and Eiffel,[2] everything in the system is an object; the approach is consistently applied. Let us consider some of the key concepts of object-oriented programming.

ENCAPSULATION

One of the most important characteristics of object-oriented programming systems is that they achieve a higher degree of modularity than previous styles of programming.[3] This is because of their encapsulation of data and function. In older languages, although a certain degree of modularity is possible through the use of subroutines, there is still a significant chance for interference between modules because these modules generally share a common pool of data. The result is that one module often changes the data or its

---

[2] There are also hybrid systems such as the popular C++, which has some of the features of object orientation and lacks others. Most of this discussion pertains to the pure object-oriented languages, and especially to Smalltalk, with which I am most familiar.

[3] At least, they *can* achieve it. It is perfectly possible to write spaghetti code in an object-oriented language, just as it is possible to write elegantly modular code in a traditional language. It is simply harder in each case.

format is such a way as to confuse or make meaningless another module's use of that same data.4

In object-oriented languages, by contrast, each object's data is encapsulated along with its own methods, and care is taken not to allow other objects to interfere with that data. Object-oriented languages thus provide programming some of the benefits that property rights provide economies. Indeed, Mark Miller and Eric Drexler hold that the development of object-oriented programming constitutes an independent rediscovery by programmers of the virtues of property rights.5 Just as property rights secure to economic agents a sphere of autonomy, and a confidence that the possessions for which they make plans will not be interfered with arbitrarily from the outside, encapsulation provides software objects an autonomy and the security that the data they depend on will not be interfered with. The upshot is similar in both settings: just as property rights foster coordination in the economy, encapsulation fosters coordination in the development of software systems.

Encapsulation provides those involved in the learning process with two big advantages. First is support for a clear division of knowledge. The second is greater understandability of the evolving system, through letting us understand it in meaningful chunks (this assumes, of course, that the objects are appropriately chosen!)

---

4 This problem of unwanted interference with shared data bears a close resemblance with a well-known problem in economics with communal property. We call it "the tragedy of the commons." The commons, in late feudal times, was the grazing land on which the lord of the area allowed the peasants to feed their cattle and sheep. As the population grew and the number of animals began to exceed the capacity of the land to feed them all, a problem arose: the farmers overused and ruined the commons. It was a simple matter of incentives. Because the commons was used in common, each farmer received all the benefit of his animals' grazing, but bore only his proportional share of the cost in degraded grazing land. No farmer had any individual incentive to reduce his herds' grazing, because he could not exclude others, whose herds would eat the grass that his did not. As a result, commons lands around Britain were badly harmed. Only when they were enclosed (encapsulated)—made into private property—was the problem solved. A private owner can exclude outside interference and thereby gain the benefits of careful management of a resource.

5 See Miller and Drexler (1988) for a provocative discussion of this idea.

MESSAGE PASSING

In object-oriented programming, encapsulation is supported by a means of intermodule communication called *message passing*. Each method that an object "knows how" to carry out can be triggered by that object's receiving a corresponding message. If the object "understands" the message—that is, if it has a corresponding method in its repertoire of functionality—it performs that method. (If not, it triggers an error message in the system and the programmer gets to do some debugging.) In no other way can one object in a system interact with another. Message passing thus enforces the division of labor among objects.

In this respect, message passing is reminiscent of contracting in the economy: we don't direct our accountant or plumber in doing his or her work, we simply send a message requesting some service he or she can perform.

Message passing also serves an important security function: one part of a program simply cannot interfere with data encapsulated in another. It has no means for doing so. All it can do is send an appropriate message asking for, say, some part of that data or that an operation be performed on it.

POLYMORPHISM

One of object-oriented technology's most powerful means of helping programmers manage complexity is polymorphism. Though the name is daunting, the concept is an entirely familiar one from everyday life. Polymorphism is the assignment of the same name to different but related actions. If, for example, I were to ask you to shut the window, and then ask you to shut the door, you would not be confused. You would interpret 'shut' in two different, though related, ways appropriate to the two different contexts. Windows are shut with a different set of actions than doors are shut. In like manner, object-oriented programming languages interpret the same method name in different manners appropriate to the context, that is, appropriate to what kind of object is involved. That is polymorphism.

As simple as it sounds, it has been tremendously empowering to programmers. No longer do they need to compose different

names for each slightly different action in slightly different contexts. They use the same appropriate term in all contexts, but
implement the methods differently for each kind of object. With
polymorphism, programmers can address the great complexity of
dealing with many slightly different kinds of objects by the simpli-
fying power of abstraction, as we do in everyday life with our various different meanings for 'shut' (shut off the TV; shut the book;
shut up). Polymorphism lets us avoid addressing complexity with
complicatedness, as we must in programming languages that
require a different kind of 'shut' for each context (for example,
`shut_window, shut_door, shut_tv, shut_mouth...`).

Polymorphism dramatically facilitates the social learning process of capital development by helping those involved both understand what they are doing and also communicate easily with one
another, by making good use of the mind's ability to abstract.

INFORMATION HIDING

Polymorphism and message passing make possible *information hiding*. Information hiding has to do not with secrecy, as it might
sound, but with fostering the division of knowledge. It does so by
making it unnecessary for programmers or objects to have much
information about the other objects with which they interact. The
key point is that all a programmer or object needs to know about
another object is what useful services it can provide and what messages it must be sent to trigger those services. It is not necessary to
know anything about *how* the object actually does what it does.

The analogy to everyday life is strong. When we deal with an
accountant, for example, we might ask her (send her the message)
to figure out our tax liability on a certain transaction. All we need
to know is what message to send her to get her to perform the
desired service. We do not know, nor do we want to know, exactly
how she does it. That would defeat the whole purpose of the division of labor. It would distract us with unnecessary knowledge, and
might lead us to give the accountant unwanted advice as to how to
do her job.

Another benefit of information hiding is interchangeability of
implementation. When a programmer works out an improved

method for some kind of object, she can simply pull out the old implementation and put in the new. As long as the message that triggers it remains the same, no one else need know, and no other kinds of objects need be changed; changes in one module necessitate corresponding changes in other modules far less frequently in object-oriented programming than in conventional programming. Hence information hiding is an important enabler of software evolution.

CLASSES AND INHERITANCE

In object-oriented programming, every object in a program or system is an object of a particular kind or class. As such, it is called an instance of that class. Classes themselves are an important kind of abstraction, called *abstract data type*. There can be thousands of instances of a certain class within a particular system, or none. Class is the abstraction, the kind of object. With the help of classes, which abstract from the particular characteristics of particular objects what those kinds of objects all share, programmers have another means of getting a grip on complexity.

Furthermore, classes are organized in inheritance hierarchies, which help make clear what kinds of things they are and allow the sharing of characteristics. David Taylor explains classes and inheritance as follows:

> *Inheritance* is a mechanism whereby one class of objects can be defined as a special case of a more general class, automatically including the methods . . . of the general class. Special cases of a class are known as *subclasses* of that class; the more general class, in turn, is known as the superclass of its special cases. In addition to the methods . . . they inherit, subclasses may define their own methods and . . . may override any of the inherited characteristics. (1990, p. 22)

For example, we might have the general class of objects *vehicle,* with subclass *fourWheeledVehicle,* which in turn has subclasses *car* and *truck.* Classes *car* and *truck* would inherit all the methods of *fourWheeledVehicle* and *vehicle,* but each could specialize any of these methods as appropriate, and add additional methods as needed.

In David Taylor's words,

> The invention of the class hierarchy is the true genius of object-oriented technology. Human knowledge is structured in just this manner, relying on generic concepts and their refinement into increasingly specialized cases. Object-oriented technology uses the same conceptual mechanisms we employ in everyday life to build complex yet understandable software systems. (1990, p. 24)

SUMMARY

Dramatic improvements in computer hardware have relaxed the resource constraints that shaped programming practice in the early days. Relatively freed from resource constraints and increasingly ambitious in undertaking large, complex problems, software developers found themselves confronting a daunting complexity constraint—maintaining coordination in an increasingly distributed learning process so as to manage the complexity of the systems they were trying to build. In response to this challenge, a variety of tools and development methodologies have evolved to enable better abstraction capability, more modularity of system design, and better conceptual grasp of the evolving systems. The recent development of object-oriented technology has provided substantial advances in programmers' ability to manage complexity with effective modularity and abstraction.

Designing New Software Capital

Oh, I see the crescent promise of my spirit hath not set.
Ancient founts of inspiration well through all my fancy yet.

—Tennyson, "Locksley Hall"

In speaking with each other we constantly pass over into the
thought world of the other person; we engage him, and he engages
us. So we adapt ourselves to each other in a preliminary way
until the game of giving and taking—the real dialogue—begins.

—Hans-Georg Gadamer (1975, p. 57)

INTRODUCTION

WE HAVE SEEN THAT CAPITAL GOODS are, in their essence, embodied knowledge. In this chapter we look at the implications of this insight for the software development process. We investigate the process of new software development, its problems, practices, and historical developments, and account for what we find in terms of this essential nature of capital.[1] We will see that because capital is

---

[1] We need to keep in mind that virtually all capital goods are used jointly with others. Hence we will try to think about individual capital goods in terms of the contexts in which they are used, and think of software applications as systems of sub-programs that interact extensively with one another. Most software constitutes not so much a single tool as a system of tools (Consider a word processor, for example. It has many modules including its text editor, printer drivers, spelling checker, search and replace facilities, and so on).

knowledge, new software development is a social learning process, and we will identify important aspects of that process.

In an effort to get a good grasp on the software development process as a whole, we will take two different perspectives on it. We focus first on its *social* aspect—its necessarily interpersonal nature—through an examination of evolving software development practice. Then we focus on its being a *learning* process—one in which knowledge grows, becomes coherent and embodied in a usable form—through examining the evolving high-order goods used in the process, that is, the tools software engineers have developed to help them in their work. In the next chapter we will go on to consider the challenge of software maintenance, focusing on software development being an ongoing, never-completed *process* that occurs through time. Inevitably we will cover some of the same ground from different angles. Such repetition should be useful because the software development process, like a software system itself, is a complex system beyond our complete understanding, but which we can understand better and better by taking a variety of different views into it.

DISCOVERING WHAT THE SOFTWARE MUST "KNOW": WHY PROTOTYPING

That capital is embodied knowledge has at least two profound implications for the software development process. First, because that knowledge is originally dispersed among many people, the development process must include and draw from those many people in some way. In other words, the development process is inevitably a *social* process, involving a number of people who must interact for the process to succeed. Second, because much of that knowledge is tacit rather than articulate, and also because it is not clear at the outset what knowledge is relevant, the development process must draw the knowledge out of them rather than simply ask them to state it. In other words, it is a *learning* process rather than a simple information transfer.

Much traditional software methodology has ignored these two facts about the knowledge that becomes software. In particular they have ignored the second, and assumed that the necessary knowledge could be identified and clearly articulated at the outset. Failures of immense proportions have resulted.

The software development community has been learning from these failures, however,[2] and better approaches have been evolving in recent years. These approaches use various techniques aiming to discover what knowledge is relevant—what needs and opportunities a new software tool may address, and how. Important among these techniques is *prototyping*. The prototyping process constitutes a kind of dialogue in which all the various people whose knowledge must be embodied in the new capital participate.[3] The medium for the dialogue is the prototype itself—the emerging design. In a sense it is the prototype itself that learns, rather than the human participants, because it is in the prototype alone that all the relevant knowledge may be found in useful form.

CAPTURING DIVIDED, TACIT KNOWLEDGE

Mark Mullin begins his 1990 book *Rapid Prototyping for Object-Oriented Systems* with this loose definition of rapid prototyping:

> This book deals with the concept of *rapid prototyping*, a process where specifications for a piece of software are developed by interaction between a *software developer*, a *client,* and a *prototype program.* Rapid prototyping is used when a client cannot initially define the requirements for a piece of software to a degree necessary to satisfy more traditional design methodologies, such as those defined by Edward Yourdon and Michael Jackson. (p. xi)

---

[2] This is to say, market evolution is gradually selecting out the bad techniques and selecting in the better.

[3] Joint application design (JAD) and rapid application development (RAD) are related approaches. Joint application design stresses bringing together all the people who should make a contribution to the design; rapid application development involves a combination of joint application design sessions, CASE tools, and prototyping. For our purposes, what is crucial to all these is the interactive learning at which they aim.

There is a sharp distinction between the prototyping approach and traditional methodologies in respect to the assumptions made about knowledge in the software development process—who knows what, when, and in what manner. Traditional methodologies implicitly view the relevant knowledge as articulable and static. M. F. Smith points to three assumptions these methodologies share.

> The first assumption is that all the requirements and needs of applications can be analysed and understood adequately by the users and software developers before development begins. . . . There is also an assumption . . . that software needs and requirements will be stable. . . . Finally, there is an assumption . . . that users understand fully the technical documentation presented to them. (1991, p. 4)

The prototyping approach, in contrast, recognizes that the necessary knowledge is far more elusive, changing, and difficult to communicate. Perhaps most importantly, the clients for whom the software tool is being designed do not know what they want, or at least they are unable to say what that is. Much of the users' knowledge, like much knowledge in general, is tacit, inarticulate. Accordingly, the most fundamental kind of knowledge necessary to the tool-building process—what the tool is to do—is not readily accessible at the outset. As Mullin puts it,

> Unfortunately, clients rarely have this complete a grasp on their problem; they usually assume their responsibilities are simpler, namely, they:
> - Recognize that a problem exists
> - Find an expert to solve the problem (1990, p. xi)

Nobody is clear about just what the problem is. But if the clients cannot say what sort of tool they want built, how are the tool builders to find out? Prototyping provides a means. Prototyping is an iterative process that accommodates adjustment and change; it anticipates instability of requirements.

> Requirements and software actually evolve together through-out the lifecycle of the project. . . . In the iterative approach to

software development, users "stay in the loop," refining their requirements as they better understand what application features are possible . . . (Adams 1992b, p. 7)

The prototype itself serves as a valuable communication medium through which designers and users can reach reasonable confidence that they understand one another. Because the process is iterative, it allows for frequent, regular interaction. Because the prototype is a version of the evolving tool, the dialogue has a clear, mutually understandable focus. Instead of having to make sense of a lengthy requirements document and evaluate whether that written description really captures what they want (or think they want), users can interact directly with the prototype and experience whether or not it meets or fails to meet their needs.

It is perhaps understandable that traditional methodologies assume well-understood, fixed requirements. The computer field is very young, and many early programs were essentially electronic replications of existing manual systems such as inventory management and accounts payable. In these kinds of cases, knowledge of the tool's function is mostly available. The users know pretty well what they want and express it reasonably clearly. The software designers have the added help of being able to look at what is being done on paper. In such circumstances, it was not so necessary for developers and users to carry on a dialogue through which they could come to understand one another.

But the old methodologies are severely strained under present conditions. Today,

> [s]oftware developers are no longer confronting situations where they are reproducing manual systems. Now they are expected to replace a chunk of the client's middle management with an expert system, one that uses all of the system's existing data to decide such things as when to reorder, how much to reorder, what bills to pay, and what customers are good credit risks.
>
> . . . [The designer may sometimes] be lucky enough to get a clear definition of the problem and be able to see an immediate solution. . . . More often, a client will say something like, "Gee, this system has completely changed the way we do

business. And now we have all of these great ideas about how
we can get the system to do even more for us." Unfortunately
they can't give you a lot of detail about these new ideas. After
all, that's why they hired you. (Mullin 1990, pp. 2-3)

A new software system's requirements cannot be fully known,
and hence the software's capabilities cannot be fully specified, at
the project's inception. In this lies the problem with traditional
methodologies based on the classical "waterfall" model, in which
design begins after the software requirements are (supposedly)
fully specified and analyzed.

> [T]he conventional "waterfall" methodology practiced in most
> large companies today . . . requires the creation and approval
> of numerous detailed documents before the first procedure is
> ever written . . . [and] doesn't allow any modifications once the
> actual programming has begun. This constraint frustrates
> [client] managers to no end because they rarely know what
> they really want until they see it running on a screen, at which
> point it's too late to make any changes! (Taylor 1990, p. 97)

The difficulty of this approach is illustrated in the experience
of one developer working on a project that was to provide "the
usual project deliverables of requirements specification, functional
specification, and design specification which cover the specification phase of a development project." They found that

> [t]he functional specification standard . . . was too inflexible
> for the needs of the GUI [the graphical user interface they
> were building]. Other techniques such as formal specification
> were inappropriate considering the time constraints.
>
> Thus a more pragmatic approach was accepted—that of
> prototyping. (Barn 1992, p. 25)

The point of rapid prototyping is to establish the requirements, to find out what the tool must do. "Your job as a rapid prototyper," says Mullin, "is to work with the client to extract specifications for their new software." Early in the process, your focus "is
simply on defining *why* this software is being written in the first
place, which will tell you *what* is expected of it" (1990, pp. 214–215).

Among certain members of the mainstream CASE community, the significant and ongoing challenge of establishing what software systems are to do is now being recognized. In "A Self-Assessment by the Software Engineering Community," summarizing the findings of the International Workshop on Computer-Aided Software Engineering, Ronald Norman and Gene Forte write that "Prevention [of defects] begins with better ways to capture, represent, and validate the objectives and requirements of systems we are trying to build. . ." They continue: "There is still much work to be done in defining generic [software development] processes . . . Areas that are particularly weak in process definition [include] requirements elicitation. . ." (1992b, p. 29).

Requirements elicitation is a basic purpose of rapid prototyping, which takes a wholly different approach to software development from that of traditional methodologies. Simply put, rapid prototyping works as follows: After an initial meeting, the developer produces a very simple prototype that the clients can try out on the computer. Then follows a repeated sequence of the following steps:

- The clients try out the current version of the prototype and react to it. They explain as well as they can what they like and don't like. Equally important, the developers observe what the clients do and don't do, what they try, what they ignore, where they are frustrated, and where they are pleased.

- Informed with this new knowledge, the developer improves and extends the prototype, and offers this new version to the clients for trial.

The cycle continues in a kind of dialogue—a conversation in which the prototype itself is passed back and forth, as much as any words about it—until the prototype has been refined to where it contains the functionality the client needs. At that point the initial version of the software to be delivered is defined, and the developer's emphasis turns to details of implementation. (This transition is a change in emphasis, rather than a switch from one set of activities to a distinctly different set. Analysis, design, and implementation are really occurring together throughout the software development process.)

The growth of prototyping in software development is a tacit recognition in the software industry that knowledge is more tacit and more dispersed than has previously been recognized. The change from the traditional, "waterfall"-type methodologies to methodologies that depend on prototyping seems to represent a shift in view of software development. It is seen less and less as a matter of manipulating static knowledge and more and more as a matter of dynamic learning.

KNOWLEDGE OF FUNCTION, KNOWLEDGE OF DESIGN, KNOWLEDGE OF IMPLEMENTATION

At this point, let us step back and look at the software development process from a broad perspective. There seem to be three general aspects to the process, corresponding to three broad categories of knowledge that must be brought to bear in the process: knowledge of function, of design, and of implementation.[4]

1. *Establishing requirements.*   What is the software to do? What is this tool supposed to be able to accomplish? This knowledge of function comes primarily from the tool user.

2. *Design.*   What sort of tool may be fashioned so as to provide the desired functionality? What sort of design would best meet the users' requirements? This knowledge of design comes primarily from the designer, the specialist tool-maker.

3. *Implementation.*   This is the detailing of the design, the coding process. How, precisely, is this design realized? How may the details of construction be arranged so as to achieve good performance in speed and efficient use of machine resources? This knowledge of implementation comes primarily from the skilled programmer.

---

[4] We pointedly do not call these "stages," because they do not and cannot occur in sequence. They cannot be sharply partitioned either in time or in the nature of the development activity. "Final implementation," for instance, nearly always involves elements of design, as the programmer figures out the best way to implement a particular algorithm; and "design" encompasses many high-level implementation decisions.

Prototyping is valuable in software development because it serves to bring out all these kinds of knowledge, which are often not only dispersed and tacit, but also *latent*. Some of those whose knowledge needs to be incorporated in the software may not be consciously aware of their knowledge; that knowledge may be latent, in need of being brought out in application to the problem at hand. The dialogical process of prototyping serves to trigger the rediscovery or creation of useful knowledge on the part of the participants. The users' reactions stimulate the design knowledge of the designer, and the functionality offered in successive versions of the prototype stimulates the users' knowledge of function, helping them become more clear as to what the tool needs to do. Furthermore, the prototype itself provides the medium in which these different kinds of knowledge may be captured.

Knowledge of implementation, finally, often resides in still others, the actual coders. Once the clients accept the prototype as offering what they need, the designer often turns over the implementation job to programmers who specialize in efficiency of implementation: they construct the design to run with the best possible balance of high speed and low memory use on the computers for which it is intended.[5]

As we have seen, prototyping often serves to draw out clients' tacit knowledge, knowledge they have, but cannot state. Even when they seem to know at some level, often they cannot express it. The prototyper discovers this knowledge by showing them different capabilities and carefully attending to their responses. Significantly, however, it is not clients alone who have knowledge they cannot articulate: much of the designers' knowledge is tacit as well. They cannot say precisely what makes good design, nor why they take some steps rather than others. Prototyping provides designers a process they can use to draw from themselves their latent knowledge of how different kinds of challenges should be

---

[5]The kinds of knowledge involved in design and in implementation are not independent, because designers must know what it is possible to implement, and implementors essentially design the details of their implementation. Nevertheless, these two types of knowledge are conceptually distinct and may not be concentrated in the same person.

approached, without committing too early to design decisions difficult to change later.

In addition to being dispersed and tacit, the knowledge valuable to a software development project is generally *incomplete*. It accumulates continually over time. This is why prototyping must be iterative. Each time designers listen to feedback from their clients, their knowledge of the clients' wants increases, and each time the clients interact with a prototype, their knowledge of the software's potential increases. In this manner grows the knowledge necessary to building a software tool.

SOFTWARE DEVELOPMENT AS INTERACTIVE LEARNING

Because the different knowledge that must ultimately be incorporated in a new software application is dispersed, tacit, and incomplete, the development of new software capital is necessarily a discovery procedure, an *interactive* learning process. Through the interaction of all those who have the knowledge the software needs, that dispersed knowledge is brought together in the new software tool. The knowledge gets built into, coalesces in, becomes embodied in, the software.

Thus, in an important sense, it is actually the tool itself—the new software—that "learns." The client never learns what the designer knows of modularity and information hiding; the designer never fully understands the client's management style to which he is tailoring the system; the programmers never learn why the screens must look like *this* instead of like *that*. The only place in which all the relevant knowledge truly resides is the software itself.[6]

In this view, the development of new capital goods can be seen as a prime instance of the social cooperation of the market process. Just as the farmer, miller, and baker cooperate in producing bread for others to consume, so the client, designer, and programmer cooperate in producing new software tools for the client (and others) to use in further production. The knowledge inputs of all

---

[6]For an intriguing explication of the complex interdependencies of our knowledge, and the degree to which we unknowingly draw on a tremendous amount of shared knowledge and understanding in our routine activities, see Phil Salin' s article on " The Wealth of Kitchens" (1990).

are necessary, and the only "place" where they exist together is in the bread or the software. Anyone who eats the bread or uses the software thereby takes advantage of the knowledge contributions of all those who have participated in its production.

The learning process of software development is evolutionary and non-deterministic; it cannot be automated, and it defies capture in a rigid methodology. Traditional approaches to software development seem to make the same kind of assumption that is made in many neo-classical economic models: that all the relevant knowledge is available, and that therefore what remains is to work out its consequences mechanically, optimizing within given constraints. In this error we can see both why traditional approaches to software engineering have led to cost overruns and frustrations for clients and developers, and why neo-classical economics is inadequate for illuminating the software development process. As Mullin says,

> I have stressed that modern software development often has little resemblance to the formal development process taught in schools and industry accepted texts. Instead, it's much more of a hit-or-miss affair, with everyone stumbling around in the dark, hoping that they will trip over the correct solution to the problems confronting them. This arises primarily from the fact that software development is innately a human process, as opposed to the mechanistic process many claim it to be. If such an argument were true there wouldn't be much need for programmers, as our current technology is well suited for automating mechanical tasks. When the task requires creativity and insight, our technology is of little use. (1990, p. 136)

Mullin overstates here. It is not that our technology is of little use, but that we must use it differently when we are learning than when we are mechanically applying what we have learned.

Let us look more closely at the nature of this learning process as illustrated by rapid prototyping. Inevitably the process is interactive, because the relevant knowledge of function and design are dispersed and must be brought together.

Interaction between User and Designer

In a discussion of a product they built for Hewlett-Packard, Bob Whitefield and Ken Auer of Knowledge Systems Corporation bring out the inescapable necessity of interaction between client and designer. The product, the Hierarchical Process Modeling System (HPMS), provides computer automation for Hierarchical Process Modeling (HPM), Hewlett-Packard's means of modeling its internal business and manufacturing processes. Whitefield and Auer explain that they rejected one development possibility because "the development time and costs were prohibitive considering the immature state of the HPM methodology. What was needed was a quick and inexpensive prototype *to continue exploring what kind of tool HP really needed*" (Whitefield and Auer 1991, p. 65, emphasis added). Because Hewlett-Packard was still developing HPM, clearly they were unable to define it fully for Knowledge Systems. The methodology and the computer tool that was to represent it were to co-evolve in an exploratory process of interaction between client and software designer.

As a specific illustration of this interaction, consider the following excerpt from Whitefield and Auer's description:

> In addition to its graphical representation, each component also has a semantic counterpart. It is entirely possible to create and edit models using only textual browsers, but few users ever do so. In fact, users spend so much of their time using the construction diagram that they tend to think of the diagram itself as the model. As the key nature of the construction diagram became apparent, the following requirements were established for the final tool . . . (1991, p. 67)

"Became apparent" is the revealing phrase here. The users of HPMS at Hewlett-Packard did not specify at the outset that, for their purposes, a picture was worth a thousand words. The designers learned this through interaction with their clients. Without this interaction—suppose, for instance, Hewlett-Packard and Knowledge Systems had tried to proceed by traditional "waterfall" methodology and begin with a document containing all the software specifications—this knowledge would probably not have emerged, or at least not without a great deal of frustration, misunderstanding, and delay.

Interaction between User and Tool

Note that there is another kind of interaction at work here: that between the client and the tool itself. The reason the HPMS users did not specify the importance of the diagrams is probably that they themselves did not realize it; after all, they had never used this kind of tool. The users discovered what they wanted and needed through interaction with the tool itself, as it evolved.

Whitefield and Auer are explicit about the discovery that occurred as the users interacted with the prototypes. For example, "As the alpha version of HPMS began to be used, response time was determined to be a critical factor in user acceptance. A goal of less than two seconds to route and draw most diagrams was established for the final product. . ." Also, "HP often desired cosmetic changes to diagrams. *As experience was gained with the tool,* flaws in default placement and appearance were uncovered. This was expected, although the extent and types of changes were not" (1991 p. 67, emphasis added). The users at HP needed to use the tool to realize their speed requirements and to identify flaws in the defaults.

Two aspects of the discovery process show up in the client users' interaction with the prototype. One has to do with the nature of knowledge. Much of the users' knowledge of their work is tacit, inarticulate—they know what they do much better than they can describe it. Therefore one element of this discovery process consists of the users' discovering in the conscious, articulate part of their minds the tacit knowledge already there. In using the HPMS prototypes, for example, the users at HP bring their tacit knowledge to bear, and where the tool does not match smoothly with what they actually do, they detect problems. Of course, they need not be able to explain these problems completely. Tacit knowledge made more explicit through interaction with the prototype need not be made fully articulate, but only clear enough so that it can be communicated to the designer for incorporation into the next version of the prototype.

Another, more subtle aspect of the discovery process has to do with the incompleteness of knowledge. We have examined bringing to light already existing, inarticualte knowledge. In some sense, the users of a prototype know that they want and need certain capabilities in the software, but they are unable to express these needs to the designers. Now, by contrast, we consider the discovery of capabilities that the users do *not* want or need at the outset, because those capabilities never occur to them in any manner. Only in working with the prototype do they first conceive of these capabilities. Once they do conceive of them, however, they want them.

The working prototype provides a context in which previously unimagined possibilities can come to mind. One programmer and tester of new software says, "When I try out a new user interface, I find myself trying to do things with it. When it won't let me, I'm frustrated." The interface—what the users see of the prototype—suggests possibilities to the users. It provides them with a new way to look at what they do, and this look may generate new insights as to what they *might* do.

The tacitness and incompleteness of the users' knowledge of what they need are the main reasons for the failure of traditional methodologies in modern software development. Software requirements cannot be articulated completely in the first stages of development because the necessary knowledge is incomplete and because much of it is inarticulate. Only through interacting with the developing tool do users discover and communicate to designers what they need.

Interaction between Designer and Tool

But it is not only the users who interact with the tool, of course; the designers do also. This may seem so obvious as not to need mention: how could the designers ever produce their designs without interacting with them? The point to be stressed, however, concerns the nature of this interaction: the designers themselves are engaged in an evolutionary subprocess of generating the new knowledge that constitutes the evolving design. They are learning also, not just about what the client needs, but about what they themselves can do. Ward Cunningham, a widely-respected programmer, designer, and methodologist, describes some of his design experience in these terms:

We'd get an idea, type it in, and say "Let's see what that does."
Kent would ask me a question. I would say, "I don't know,"
but I'd just start typing and we'd let the machine tell us.7

Designers' knowledge of design principles and various problem-
solving techniques is not all ready to hand,8 nor is it static and
complete. They discover how to apply this knowledge to new
problems in the process of applying it. They ponder, they sketch,
they experiment, they try out various ways of decomposing the
problem, they make some initial decisions, they repeat the process.
They learn by doing. In Mullin's description, software design is
fundamentally a matter of learning.

> The best way to do OO program design is to realize that you
> are dealing with systems, and the best source of information is
> the system you are duplicating or enhancing. Your job is not
> to dictate how the system will work, but to understand how
> the system already works. As you do this, you are acquiring
> valuable information about the classes you will need to con-
> struct your system and how instances of these classes interact
> with each other at runtime. (1990, p. 36)

A good illustration of the manner in which the designer learns
through working with the design comes in Mullin's description of
the initial laying out of the views (screens) that the user will see.

> The actual act of laying out the view provides you with another
> set of information you will need in constructing the prototype.
> By deciding on the visual grouping of information in the view,
> you will also be determining any data assembly, or aggregation,
> capabilities that the view needs. (1990, p. 28)

By laying out a view, you learn something; by deciding on
grouping, you determine needed capabilities. In brief, by interacting with the evolving design the designer learns more about what
it should be.

7Personal interview conducted October 1992. " Kent" is Kent Beck, a respected Smalltalk consul-
tant and president of First Class Software.

8But see the discussion of design patterns below.

A creative process such as software design is not deterministic, with output dictated by input through some sort of black-box optimization. This would require the designer to grasp the problem in its entirety at a glance, and on that basis to grasp its "correct" solution. On the contrary, software design is an evolutionary process in which the designer "makes sense" of the problem over time, and gradually puts the design together. In this respect software design would seem to be akin to writing. Composition is not a matter of copying out a book that has somehow popped into the writer's head. Rather the writer works gradually from a vague idea to a fully-conceived book, through a process of fleshing out, defining and refining, finding out what works by trial and error. Similarly, the software designer uses feedback from the design itself, seeing what works, what has promise, what relationships are revealed that were unclear before.

Iteration: The Design Dialogue

We have discussed interaction between client and designer, and interaction between both of these and the prototype itself. These two kinds of interaction are closely related in practice, even the same in a sense, because it is largely by means of their interaction with the prototype that the two groups interact with each other. The prototype is a communication medium. Those involved communicate with one another largely in their responses to the prototype, with these responses closely observed by the other side. In a sense, there is a dialogue going on in which the prototype is passed back and forth. The designers say, "Give this a try," and watch. The users try it out, experiment, exclaim about some features, pout about others, ask questions, and describe frustrations. "Well, this part is good," they say, " but that part needs to be more like so. Set up as it is, I can't do such and such." The designers, in turn, think, "So *that's* what they want! (Why didn't they say so in the first place?) Well, I can give them something twice as good as what they're asking for. Wait until they see this. . . ." In the next iteration, the user may respond, "No, no! That's not what I need! But it's marvelous! You can do that?! Well then do it this way. . . !"

This fanciful example illustrates another important characteristic of the learning process that is software development: it is *iter-*

ative. Both sides in the dialogue are learning from one another. On the basis of what they learn in each round of the exchange, they change what they feed back to the other side, thereby calling forth new learning there. The process is gradual because learning takes time. The new software develops throughout this ongoing exchange, as more and more of the necessary and appropriate knowledge gets built into it, and extraneous, unnecessary knowledge is discarded. Here is Mullin, again:

> In RP [rapid-prototyping] design, we stop designing on a regular basis in order to run the prototype by the clients and users, thereby getting information on adjusting our design before it's too late to do anything about the parts they hate, or the things they really wish it had. So, for all my arguments about seamless development environments, it appears that our design actually progresses by fits and starts, as opposed to the seamless path of traditional design evolution.
>
> As it happens, this observation is wrong. These sessions with the client are not "seams" in the RP design process, they are natural components of it. They provide us with the means to continually adjust our design course and goals as we learn more about what the client desires by letting them interact with our best idea of what it is that they do desire. As they do this, they will provide us with the necessary information to extend the design another level. Recall that I observed at the outset of this book that it wasn't realistic to expect to get a clear list of requirements from a client when you commence a design project. We are designing to the requirements we have and then using that design to dig up more requirement information. (1990, pp. 86–7)

DESIGNING AS UNDERSTANDING: THE ROLE OF TOOLS FOR THOUGHT

We concentrated in the previous section on the social, interpersonal aspects of software development, through which the dispersed and often tacit knowledge that must be built into a new application is accumulated. In this section we take a different perspective on the same process, concentrating on the learning aspects, on *how* that knowledge gets successfully articulated into working code. We do this through an examination of the higher-order tools software designers use to help them do their work of creating software tools. *The fundamental challenge in software development is to make sense of the complex systems we are trying to build:* to understand them and the way they function, and to express that understanding in code. Most of the tools software designers use (higher-level programming languages in particular) are usefully thought of as tools for helping them *understand* what they are doing.

An important and illuminating exception to this rule are automatic code generators, both those that generate higher-level code from diagrams, and compilers, which translate higher-level code into machine language. Paradoxically, although these tools in a sense produce software automatically, without any human participation, a look at their evolution, what they do and what they do not do, reinforces the fundamental point that software development is a wholly human learning process.

CASE TOOLS

Let us start with a quick look at CASE tools proper. The difference between what was hoped for from CASE, by its early enthusiasts, and what CASE actually contributes to software development, is informative. It was hoped, early on, that CASE would revolutionize software development by providing tools that would automate the process. The difficulty is that CASE enthusiasts misunderstood the process. They thought it was a matter simply of *transforming* knowledge of what a software system was intended to do into the code that would do it. Their unexamined, fatal assumption was that the knowledge they needed was available in usable form at the outset. If it were, then in principle they could use their various tools for analysis, design, and code generation to translate that knowledge, in "a step-by-step disciplined process," into the target system.

In fact, the process of software development is not simply one of transforming existing knowledge into code, it is one of *discovering and creating* knowledge, as well as transforming it into code.

Software development is not so much a process of translating knowledge as of discovering and articulating knowledge.

In short, software development can be understood as a process of coming to understand fully what a software system should be. Any software application starts as a rather sketchy, abstract conception; it finishes when this vague conception has been satisfactorily articulated in executable code.[9] Thus the process of building a piece of software is a process of coming to understand it fully in the sense of being able to articulate it in detail. Developing software is a matter of understanding fully what we are trying to achieve.

In this respect, software development is like any other design process. A bridge is fully designed only when the drawings, materials to be used, and other specifications are fully worked out. What the engineers are doing in designing a bridge is thus coming to understand it fully, so that they can articulate their design in complete detail in the appropriate code—in their case detailed drawings, materials specifications, and so on.

CASE tools were clearly intended by some to serve as translation tools. In practice, their usefulness lies in how they help software developers understand what they are doing.

The mindset of mainstream CASE methodology is illustrated in the following passage from *CASE Is Software Automation* by Carma McClure, author of several books on computer-aided software engineering. Having defined CASE as "the automation of software development," McClure expands as follows.

> CASE proposes a new approach to the *software life cycle* concept, that is based on automation. The basic idea behind CASE is to provide a set of well-integrated, labor-saving tools linking and automating all phases of the *software life cycle*. . . .
>
> Traditional software technologies are of two types: tools and methodologies. . . . Most software tools are stand-alone,

---

[9] Or, rather, it reaches a useful stage in its evolution. Because the capital structure around it evolves, this tool must evolve also, or die. In this sense, a particular application is really only finished when it is becoming obsolete, and thus not being developed any further.

mainframe-based, and concentrate on the implementation part of the *software life cycle*.

The software methodology category includes manual software development methodologies such as structured analysis, structured design, and structured programming. These methodologies define a *step-by-step disciplined process* for developing software.

The CASE technology is a *combination* of software tools and methodologies. Furthermore, CASE is different from earlier software technologies because it focuses on the entire software productivity problem, not just on implementation solutions. Spanning all phases of the *software life cycle,* CASE is the most complete software technology yet. CASE attacks software productivity problems at both ends of the *life cycle* by automating many analysis and design tasks, as well as program implementation and maintenance tasks.

Because manual structured methodologies are too tedious and labor intensive, *in practice they are seldom followed to the most detailed level.* CASE makes manual structured methodologies practical to use by automating the drawing of structured diagrams and the *generation of system documentation.* (1989, pp. 5–6, emphasis added)

There are a number of points here worthy of note. One is the acceptance of the idea of the traditional "software life cycle," which begins with analysis of the problem domain, and proceeds sequentially in a "a step-by-step disciplined process" through design and implementation stages. There are two important hidden assumptions here. The first is that the problem is known and awaits our analysis. The second is that implementation—actually writing code to solve the problem—properly occurs after analysis and design are completed. In this regard "the generation of system documentation" is also important. Traditional methodologies depend on extensive documentation of requirements and specification which are supposedly to be completed before coding begins.

Also noteworthy is the comment that "in practice [the structured methodologies] are seldom followed to the most detailed level." This is undoubtedly due in some measure to the tedium and labor intensity to which McClure calls attention, but it is probably also because of the developers' awareness, conscious or unconscious, that because requirements and their corresponding specifications are never really finalized, by the time they could actually complete a structured design, the requirements would have changed and they would lose their labor.

A survey of the main features offered in current CASE tools[10] reveals the following ten basic functions, grouped under four headings:

Diagramming Support

1. draw diagrams
2. check diagram consistency

Data Management

3. provide requirements database and requirements tracing
4. provide data dictionary
5. provide repository management (for workgroups)
6. support change management and version control

Prototyping Support

7. prototype (usually "screen prototyping")
8. paint screens

Code Generation

9. provide facilities for porting between platforms
10. generate code

With the exception of the last category (which we take up below in the section on automatic programming), each kind of tool serves, in its own way, to help the designers learn about the systems they are building.

The diagramming tools produce data flow diagrams, entity relationship diagrams, or program structure diagrams; or they do modeling—systems requirements modeling, data modeling, behavioral modeling. All of these visualizations are aids to designers'

---

[10]This particular listing is drawn from Kara (1992).

understanding of the complex system they are creating. And, of course, where a team is doing the development, the diagrams help maintain coordination among the team members by giving them a shared focus for discussion and a helpful visualization of what others are doing.

The tools for checking diagram consistency provide important feedback to the designers from the evolving design embodied in the diagrams. Automated diagram consistency checkers point out all the places where a version of the design is inconsistent or nonsensical, that is, where the designers have not fully grasped all the ramifications of their actions. For example, sometimes designers will indicate all the inputs necessary to a particular module but fail to specify any output. Diagram consistency checkers point out such flaws automatically.

The data management tools serve primarily to help maintain coordination among the members of a development team. Modern software development is very much a social process, as we have seen, depending on the contributions of many. In this context it is very helpful to have a shared database where a variety of information about the project can be stored and accessed. Because the requirements of a system gradually develop and change as the system takes shape, it is often helpful to have a history of their evolution, so that team members may understand why something is being done as it is. Repositories are databases where segments of code, modules of the system, can be stored and accessed by different members of the team. And, of course, as changes are made and different versions of the system are developed, it is important that coordination be maintained to avoid conflicts and inconsistent expectations. In a general way, the information provided by the various CASE databases helps the developers understand what is happening, to grasp the nature of the system they are developing, so that they may contribute their own knowledge to it.

We discussed the value of prototyping in aiding learning in the previous section and need not repeat at length here: it helps designers understand the needs of users and users understand the operation of the evolving system, so that both may better understand what the system can and should be.

All these tools are tools for learning, for making sense both of what one has done on one's own and of what others on the same team have done, and how that affects the whole. This kind of conceptual development is the designer's bread and butter.

> If you watch how a designer works you see lots of things going on which give you some insight into the thought processes going on. Sometimes a designer is just trying out some new idea. Sometimes a designer is evaluating or making some catastrophic change to previous ideas (maybe about 90 percent of the pictures a designer draws get thrown away). Sometimes a designer is trying to customise [sic] something developed for another purpose. Sometimes two designers who have developed separate pieces of a solution are trying to bring them together. Sometimes a designer is checking that all of the ideas actually hang together. One thing you will see is that very little time is actually spent on the finished product. (Robinson 1992, p. 4)

OBJECT-ORIENTED PROGRAMMING ENVIRONMENTS

Object-oriented programming environments such as Smalltalk provide some additional tools not included in the above list of standard CASE functionality. (Smalltalk and similar environments are not generally called CASE tools, even though they are wonderful instances of computer-assisted software engineering in the simple meaning of the term.) The nature of these tools also points to the learning aspects of software development and suggests why Smalltalk is such a good language for prototyping.

One of the most useful and important aspects of Smalltalk is that any chunk of code, no matter how small, can be run—and produce meaningful results—at any time. "Smalltalk is an incremental environment. Small, incremental changes are small efforts."[11] This incremental compiling capability is in marked contrast to earlier programming languages, in which the whole program has to be complete and accurate before it can be run. The importance of incremental compiling to learning has to do with the complexity of software—we may think we know what a piece of code does and

---

[11]Ward Cunningham, personal interview, October 1992.

how it interacts with other pieces, but often we don't. In developing a system, it is extremely useful to check in with reality at regular intervals, to make sure we understand. The ability to run each module of Smalltalk and look at the results gives programmers the benefit of rapid feedback from the system; it allows them to understand it better and sooner. As one programmer puts it, "your thought processes don't get interrupted; you don't leave the context."[12] Additionally, incremental compiling leads to higher quality, because smaller chunks of code are easier to test.

A related capability of Smalltalk is a built-in debugger. This is a tool for tracing exactly what happens, step by step, so that when an error occurs or something unexpected happens, the programmer can find the cause of the problem easily. This capability also provides rapid feedback and, hence, clearer understanding. Ward Cunningham says this is a large part of the reason why Smalltalk is such a good development environment.

> There was never a risk of a bad bug, because whenever something went wrong, we'd get a notifier [debugger], hop in the notifier, and it would tell us what went wrong. We were never in a position where we didn't know the next thing to do to diagnose our programs.[13]

It is important that the ongoing interaction between the designer and the design not be interrupted too long. Less-capable languages cannot tell a programmer where something went wrong, only that it did. In these circumstances it is possible to be absolutely stumped. When that happens, the programmer then has to search for the problem. In so doing, he loses the context; his thought processes get interrupted. Additionally, the whole program usually has to be recompiled and rerun before he can make sure that he has fixed the problem correctly. The sheer time this takes is distracting; it makes it difficult for the programmer to concentrate on solving the problem before him.

---

[12]Lee Griffin of IBM, personal interview, October 1992.

[13]Personal interview, October 1992.

The combination in Smalltalk of incremental compiling and the built-in debugger is especially powerful. When one "hits a bug" in Smalltalk, a debug window appears in which one can usually fix the problem quickly and easily. This change to the program is automatically and immediately compiled and linked into the rest of the program. Accordingly, it is not necessary to go back to the beginning, recompile, and begin the program again. Instead, one can simply continue with the program in its newly repaired state, by clicking on the "Restart" button on the debug window. Smalltalk users find this feature extremely useful.[14]

Of course bugs occur in all programming, but most programming languages are ill-equipped to help developers deal with them. Traditional programming languages rely on the program being correct. They assume that the end user is the only person whose efficiency needs to be optimized and aim to give the end user the fastest possible program.

Smalltalk, in contrast, recognizes in its very design that we live in a world of error. The designers of Smalltalk took very seriously the learning challenges of designing software, and therefore provided incremental compiling and a powerful debugger to support software developers.[15] One developer enthusiastic about object-oriented languages says, "these languages talk back to you and let you know when you are doing a good job." The difference between "Smalltalk and C++ is that Smalltalk talks sooner and louder when you are doing a bad job."[16]

Smalltalk also provides tools that give users a variety of different perspectives on the code. For example, there are hierarchically structured browsers for viewing the different elements of the code in the system. In addition to providing a handy means of looking up and accessing some particular class of code, browsers significantly aid understanding of software systems by providing a

---

[14]Richard Collum, systems developer in a large Smalltalk product at First Union National Bank of North Carolina, says simply, " The restart button is the greatest thing." Personal conversation, October 1992.

[15]I am indebted to Ward Cunningham for explaining this distinction.

[16]Paul Ambrose, personal telephone conversation.

meaningful view of the relationships between different elements of the system. *Where* a piece of code is located in a browser window often carries more information than the details of the code itself. Smalltalk also provides windows which display relationships between objects, such as which kinds of objects send messages to others. It also provides windows for viewing the actual values of variables pertaining to particular elements of a system.

These different views into a complex system are very helpful in understanding it. In fact, the very value of the Smalltalk browsers and windows has stimulated the development of still other kinds of tools for many different languages. These tools give different perspectives of software systems, to make more understandable various different kinds of relationships. A complex system, by its nature, cannot be wholly understood by a particular person at one time. But it can be understood better and better in proportion to one's variety of perspectives on it. Each new perspective enriches one's understanding of the other perspectives, and hence of the system as a whole.

On this point, Mark S. Miller has said that he has reservations about tools that generate code from diagrams. He prefers tools with which

> you write the code and have it generate the diagrams. That's superior because whatever you are programming in has to express the entirety of the program, and people have found words and symbols to be superior for that purpose. But the visualizing tools do a good job of representing a slice of or aspect of the program, with different tools providing different slices.[17]

Let us turn now to tools that generate code from diagrams, and other tools that, in general, relieve the programmer of writing code. In their evolution are more interesting lessons about software development as a social learning process.

---

[17]Personal telephone conversation.

AUTOMATIC PROGRAMMING

Automatic programming is a term we hear rarely now, but it refers to an important dream of the software community. Among its descendants is the automatic code generation provided by certain CASE tools. The goal of the advocates of automatic programming was to have computers, rather than people, write programs. As Mark S. Miller explains, there are opposite opinions of its success, and each opinion, viewed from its own perspective, has validity.[18]

One view is that automatic programming was a total failure. Look around us. There are millions of people writing programs, in a process that is anything but automatic. Computers can't write programs; programming requires human imagination and creativity. On its terms, this majority view is certainly valid.

But the activity we call programming today is a different activity from that which was called programming years ago, when automatic programming was first advocated. At that time, says Miller, programming

> was largely low-level assembly hacking; for example, it was concerned about what operand was in what register of the machine. As far as that activity is concerned, the advocates of automatic programming succeeded. They succeeded in automating what programming was then.

This success is thanks to the development of compilers for higher-level languages. As Miller says it, "we now specify what computation needs to happen, and the implementation in particular machine instructions is handled by compilers." We make this specification in higher-level computer languages—languages that allow us to specify what is to happen in terms more abstract than the computer can handle directly. The compiler transforms this more abstract coding into machine code that the computer can read.

---

[18]I am indebted to Mark S. Miller as the source of most of the insights of this section and the next. Quotations are from my transcription of a telephone interview with him unless otherwise noted.

The historical change in terminology on which this disagreement turns is revealing about the very nature of software development. Miller explains:

> [T]here was an incremental and gradual transformation over time of what it means to program. The transformation was from programming's being primarily implementation-oriented to its being specification-oriented. The implementation issues that were much of the programmer's concern in the old days are now handled by compilers.

To specify is to state precisely what the program must do. In standard software engineering usage, specification occurs in a language more abstract than a programming language, typically a natural language. Miller continues,

> However, there is an extraordinary number of levels of abstraction in the program. So when we think about *specifying*, at any point in the evolution of programming languages, what we mean is conceptual activity a few levels above where our programming languages are. There's too much grungy detail in the languages for us, so we specify with higher-level abstractions. What we do when we go from specification to the current level of abstractions that our languages allow us to operate at, is *now* called implementation. A few years ago, yes, that implementation would have been seen as *specifying,* because then we had no languages that could handle that level of abstraction. But the particular tasks our term *implementation* refers to change over time, with our capacities. At any time in the evolution of programming languages, we see the level of abstraction that our languages permit us as too much grungy detail.

What we called *specification* yesterday—activity which is specification from the perspective of lower-level languages—we call *implementation* today, because today we have programming languages that allow us to capture and express that level of abstraction, with compilers to do the work of transforming that abstract expression into machine code. Over time, as programmers' essential higher-order tools of production—their programming languages—have improved, what it *means* to program has changed.

What can we learn of software development from this slice of programming history? There are at least three lessons relevant to our present purposes.

First, the human imagination is necessary in addressing the particulars of each new programming challenge. Computers cannot figure out what must be done to solve a particular new kind of challenge.[19] This kind of task is fundamentally a learning process—a matter of understanding the problem and adequately expressing a software system that can address it. For the purpose of this expression, higher-level languages that enable us to express abstractions better are very helpful. We address this point at length in the next section.

Second, today's programming in higher-level languages is a profoundly social process in that it is entirely dependent on the division of knowledge embodied in tools. Each user of a higher-level language depends, for the realization of his program in executable form, on the creativity, knowledge, and expertise of those who built the compiler he uses. Those who built the compilers have addressed for us, ahead of time, "the grungy details" of machine instructions. Their knowledge, their experience with what works well and what does not, is embodied for us in the compiler we no longer notice. Because they have taken care of lower-level automatable concerns, they free us to concentrate our efforts at higher conceptual levels.

In a category similar to that of compilers are tools for generating code from diagrams or screen representations and tools for porting a system from one kind of computer to another. Examples include graphical user interface builders, code generators offered in certain CASE tools, and some visual programming languages. In each case they let us specify what is wanted in one generally higher-level and more abstract medium and turn that specification into another medium—code more accessible to the machine (or, in the case of tools for porting between different computers, to the target machine). What all these devices have in common is that

---

[19]Perhaps profound advances in artificial intelligence will make this possible someday, but that day has not arrived.

they embody knowledge of how to transform one representation into another. They perform the transformations for us, freeing us to concentrate on the substance of what we want transformed.

A third lesson taught by this history is that as capital goods improve, there is a concurrent, complementary development in what people using the tools know and do. This is a very important species of social learning. What the relevant community—in this case the programming community—does in their everyday work advances; the community learns. Over time, the programming community has built up knowledge of how to make efficient use of raw computer resources—how to manage the grungy details of machine instructions. It has also built up knowledge about what kinds of expressive capabilities are needed in computer languages. All this knowledge has been built into a set of gradually improving languages and their related compilers. In an important sense, then, this community has learned a lot about programming. The whole community is in a sense smarter in their programming practices and tools. The change is reflected in the fact that what we mean by programming is completely different now from what it was twenty-five years ago. The change has been a social one in that the new knowledge is not to be found in particular individuals, but in the whole pattern of interaction among people, tools, and practices. Individuals don't necessarily know more—in many cases they are clearly able to be effective while knowing *less* than their predecessors—rather, the knowledge that has developed is spread throughout the community, in tools, languages and practices of which no one individual has a complete grasp.

PROGRAMMING LANGUAGES AND HUMAN DIALOGUE

There are many advantages of object-oriented languages, some of which we have discussed already, and others of which we will take up in the next chapter. In the present context—the development of new software—probably none is as important as this: the " pure" object-oriented languages such as Smalltalk let software developers design and implement with a terminology that is suitable for thinking about the problems they are trying to solve. The terminology, it is said, maintains a "proximity to the problem space." Hence these languages, and the development methodologies built around them, are not just tools for expression, but tools for thinking and learning about complex systems.

Bertrand Meyer, a leading theorist of object-oriented technology and author of the object-oriented language Eiffel, points out that traditional languages are hard to read and understand; when we look at their code, the relationships are not clear to us. This, he surmises, helps explain why diagrams are so much a part of the structured analysis and design methodologies used with non-object-oriented languages. "[A]fter all," he says,

> if you are programming in BASIC or C++ you do need higher-level tools and notations if you ever hope to explain or just understand what is going on. But . . . [w]ith object-oriented techniques, implementation becomes high level enough to cover what was traditionally covered by design or even analysis. The same notation may be applied throughout, at various levels of detail. For analysis and design, high-level facilities such as classes . . . provide the key descriptive and structuring facilities. For the final implementation, classes obtained earlier are completed with the details of the algorithms and data structure implementations. (Meyer 1991, p. 39)

The same notation may be applied throughout the development process, from high-level tasks such as analysis and design through to low-level implementation, for two reasons. First, as we have discussed, object-oriented languages, like other high-level languages, allow us to specify things in ways more removed from the concerns of the machine—at a higher level of abstraction. But object-oriented languages are additionally significant, not because they are still more abstract than other recent languages, but because they let us create our own vocabulary, tailored to the problem space as we understand it, both for thinking about the problem *and* for implementing a solution to it. Programming the solution to a problem in a language such as Smalltalk is a matter of creating objects and methods that represent, respectively, the entities we wish to model and their behavior. Meyer says

> This is the seamless property of O-O development, which yields some of the major advantages of the approach—among

others, the fact that the results of analysis and design are not lost or recorded in some obscure intermediate documents or diagrams, but fully embedded in the final delivered software. (1991, p. 39)

We have said that building new capital goods is a matter of embodying knowledge in a usable form. Object-oriented languages are effective tools for this embodiment because the terms in which they let us embody our knowledge are so similar to the terms in which we naturally develop and express that knowledge. Object-oriented languages provide software designers more immediate access to the problems they are confronting; in using terms with immediate relevance to the problem domain, they avoid loss of meaning in translation. In a sense, they shorten the conceptual distance between the knowledge that goes into the new capital good and the good itself. In much traditional structured analysis and design, designers do their thinking with diagrams, which then must be converted into code by some translation process. Object-oriented languages, in contrast, allow designers to think in understandable code, thereby providing them a more immediate grasp of the system and obviating the need for translation.

Object-oriented languages, then, help us to bridge the semantic gap between analysis, design, and implementation. There is no semantic gap because the semantics are the same throughout. In this respect, object-oriented languages are superior tools for thinking about—*learning* about—complex systems.

One important result of programming in a language that is close to natural language is that it facilitates communication among people with different kinds of knowledge that must be embodied in the software. Knowledge Systems Corporation, a major development-consultancy firm specializing in Smalltalk, has extended the object-oriented approach into a methodology (on which they are still working). They

have found, by modeling entities in terms of their behavior and interaction, that both internal software objects and external entities can be represented in such natural ways as to be accessible to non-computer professionals like users and domain experts. (Adams 1992a, p. 5)

This methodology takes the idea of software development as a social learning process to its fullest extent. In order to begin developing the Smalltalk classes that will eventually be used in prototypes and evolved into a complete, running system, the software designers at Knowledge Systems use role playing. The process is overtly social, in that various different people with different knowledge and skills are involved on the spot, and it is overtly a learning process in that it is a trial-and-error method of discovering what the important objects in the software should be and how—by what methods—they should interact with one another. Sam Adams describes their experience.

> While most methodologies rely on diagramming notations to attempt to capture and communicate complex interactions between objects, role-playing allows the designers to actually experience the behavior firsthand. This theatrical anthropomorphism has many benefits in the design process. Since designs can be "executed" very early in the process using scenarios, alternative designs can be explored easily using role-playing as a form of rapid prototyping. Designs as complex as entire manufacturing systems can be simulated in surprising detail, taking advantage of the temporal and spatial nature of role-playing that can be only poorly captured on paper. . . . An additional benefit of role-playing in design groups is that it tends to help involve everyone in the design process, regardless of their background or experience, so all participants can add their unique value to the process. (1992a, p. 6)

We are accustomed to think of programming languages and computer programs as vehicles for communication between people and computers, the means by which people tell computers what to do. But because software development is so much a social activity, languages and programs need to be equally—perhaps more so—a vehicle for communication among people. Even when programming is in fact a solitary activity, when one developer writes an entire program herself, there is great value in using higher-level, more expressive languages closer to natural languages, because these help the solitary programmer think about the problem and understand what she is doing as she works. The language helps her communicate clearly with herself as she works. When programming is done in teams, and when the program must evolve over time, the importance of clear communication is multiplied. Kent Beck writes that "[t]he cost of a piece of code over its many-year life is dominated by how well it communicates to others. . . . Every method name, every class name is an opportunity for you to communicate what is happening" (1995, p. 20). Effective software development depends on effective communication among the developers, hence those languages which best foster interpersonal communication best foster effective development.

Finally, let us offer one somewhat philosophical perspective on software development as social learning. The accessibility of object-oriented programming, the manner in which it empowers thinking about problems and expressing their solutions, demonstrates that learning occurs primarily in the context of the social world, with its shared meanings captured in language. Higher-level languages have increasingly let us move away from the mundane concerns of the machine to concentrate on more general and meaningful abstractions. Software designers using higher-level languages are much less distracted by the needs of the machine. Their attention can be focused on the needs of the system they are building, in terms of the system and not the computer. Object-oriented languages and methodologies that incorporate role-playing let us take a very large step in this direction, into the world of human discourse and imagination. In the objects and methods of object-oriented languages we have something akin to the nouns and verbs of the language of society. Accordingly, with object-oriented languages our powers of expression and understanding improve substantially, informed by the richness of meaning that comes with evolved language. Because software development is a social learning process, it becomes easier as we become better able to do our thinking in terms of the social world we live in.

INTERMEDIATE GOODS FOR DESIGNERS: REUSABLE COMPONENTS AND PATTERNS

As we saw in Chapter 1, most production involves fixed capital, or tools, used according to procedures to transform working capital

into output. So far in this chapter we have focused on the procedures of software development in the first section and its fixed
capital in the second. In this last section we take a brief look at the
working capital of software development, its intermediate goods.

The design processes of any industry improve, mature, and
become more rapid and dependable as different design elements
become proven, widely known, and used by designers. Such design
elements may be either articulated and specified (so that one can
look them up in books or manuals) or so well known by all that
specification is unnecessary. These design elements constitute a
kind of working capital for designers, intermediate goods that they
can work with and incorporate into their own designs, without
having first to develop them themselves. Like fixed capital, working capital embodies knowledge of how to accomplish some productive purpose. Fixed capital is used to transform raw and intermediate goods into the desired output; working capital is the raw
and intermediate goods transformed.

Software engineering is much poorer in working capital than
are other engineering disciplines. Both individual firms and the
industry as a whole are struggling to develop standardized, robust,
understandable elements that can be incorporated into new
designs. Generally, the discussion centers around "reusable components" or "software reuse." The industry has found it very difficult to develop such standard design elements.[20] Nevertheless, it is
worth calling attention to two important kinds of working capital
for software engineering.

Classes are one kind. Classes, in object-oriented programming,
embody knowledge of how to represent effectively certain kinds of
concepts and their behavior. Some can be used as is for many purposes; most can be customized for particular purposes. Classes
provide programmers with largely worked-out solutions to particular programming problems, in the same manner that various physical materials do for engineers working on production of physical
things. When a programmer decides, "I'll use an instance of the
class *OrderedCollection* to represent these data," she is making a

---

[20]We will take up some of the reasons for their slow evolution in chapter five.

decision directly analogous to that of the bridge designer who decides, "I'll use a steel I-beam of such and such thickness to support this weight." The already-worked-out design elements are incorporated into the new designs. Having been already worked out and defined, they need not be created afresh by designers, who "merely" incorporate them where appropriate.

Design patterns are another, recently developed kind of working capital for software designers. Patterns embody verbal descriptions of the accumulated wisdom and experience of skilled practitioners with respect to how to approach certain kinds of design challenges. The leading book on the topic at present begins its definition of design patterns in this way:

> Christopher Alexander says, "Each pattern describes a problem which occurs over and over again in our environment, and then describes the core of the solution to that problem, in such a way that you can use this solution a million times over, without ever doing it the same way twice." Even though Alexander was talking about patterns in buildings and towns, what he says is true about object-oriented design patterns. Our solutions are expressed in terms of objects and interfaces instead of walls and doors, but at the core of both kinds of patterns is a solution to a problem in a context.[21]

Patterns are very high-level inputs to the production process. They give the designer a conceptual understanding of different kinds of design challenges and provide conceptual design templates with which to address them. As such, patterns are a kind of working capital for programmers: intermediate, unfinished design goods to be customized for the purpose at hand.

Classes, design patterns, and other reusable components that can be incorporated into software design are more examples of the division of knowledge and labor through capital goods. The richer

---

[21]Erich Gamma, Richard Helm, Ralph Johnson, and John Vlissides, *Design Patterns, Elements of Reusable Object-Oriented Software* (Reading, Mass.: Addison Wesley, 1995). They quote Christopher Alexander, Sara Ishikawa, Murray Silverstein, Max Jacobson, Ingrid Fiksdahl-King, and Shlomo Angel, *A Pattern Language* (New York: Oxford University Press, 1977).

the designer's repertoire of working capital to choose from—that is to say, the more of others' knowledge that is pre-embodied for him in working capital to be customized to his purposes—the faster and better the design process can go forward.

SUMMARY

Because software, like all capital, is embodied knowledge, and because that knowledge is initially dispersed, tacit, latent, and incomplete in large measure, software development is a social learning process. The process is a dialogue in which the knowledge that must become the software is brought together and embodied in the software. The process comprises interaction between users and designers, between users and the evolving tools, and between designers and the evolving tools. It is an iterative process in which the evolving tool itself serves as the medium of communication, with each new round of the dialogue eliciting more useful knowledge from the different people involved.

As programming practice has evolved, higher-order tools have been developed to facilitate the process. Some of these, such as compilers and code generators, serve to automate the clearly understood aspects of the process. These can be seen as freeing human effort to undertake, at ever-higher levels of abstraction, the creative learning that is the essence of design. Most of the tools now used to facilitate the design process help software builders better understand the complex systems they build. The most promising of these tools are the object-oriented technologies, which allow us to create the kinds of abstractions we need both to think about the problems effectively and to specify their solutions.

Rules of thumb for software development organizations that are implied in this discussion can be summarized as follows:

Development Methodology

- Prototype rapidly, allowing for several iterations of client response to the prototype and subsequent revision. This is how you find out what the client really wants and needs.

- Make sure client users (and not just managers) are involved in the dialogue over the prototype.

- Use a methodology that is iterative, allowing analysis, design, and implementation to go together. Abandon the waterfall model.

Tools

- Choose a language that is as close to natural language as possible.

- Choose a language that facilitates substantial change to the evolving design, because changes will have to be made as those involved learn better what they want to accomplish.

- Choose a language and programming environment that makes the best use of programmer resources rather than machine resources.

- Choose a language that allows incremental compiling so that programmers get rapid, fine-grained feedback from what they are doing.

- Choose a pure object-oriented language such as Smalltalk or Eiffel.

- In programming style, emphasize clarity above all. Strive to use clear terminology that both technical and non-technical people can understand.

- Use CASE tools sparingly. Use those which help your team understand what they are doing: Avoid those that require a linear, step-by-step process.

Reusable Components

- Choose a programming environment with a rich class hierarchy built in.

- Invest in your own, company-specific reusable classes.

- Learn about and use design patterns now being developed and published.

Designing Evolvable Software

Knowledge comes, but wisdom lingers, and I linger on the shore,
And the individual withers, and the world is more and more.
                                        —Tennyson, "Locksley Hall"

. . . when you realize that much of the software problem has to do
with building very complex systems that will run on networks
with different kinds of hardware, and that no application will
be considered done when shipped, you're inescapably led to a
much more biological, modular system, for which something like
objects will be required.

                                        —Alan Kay (1992, p. 13)

INTRODUCTION

The process of software development does not end when the first
version is shipped to the customer. It continues throughout the
life of the product. The world changes, hence the software must
change with it, *if it is to maintain or increase its value as a useful capital*
good. Users' requirements change as their businesses change. The
software needs new features to keep up with competitive products.
It needs to run on new machines, to be used on networks, to drive
new printers and plotters, and so on. In the broadest view, as the
economy grows and develops through the accumulation of new
knowledge and its embodiment in new tools and new systems, software products must themselves "learn"—be enhanced by the incorporation of new knowledge—to maintain and/or improve their

position of usefulness in complement to the other elements of the evolving capital structure.

The process of adapting and enhancing existing software is known as *software maintenance*. It is challenging and costly. At present, the software industry is very concerned about maintenance problems, as evidenced by advertisements such as the following, which included a graphic of a hooded skeleton with a scythe, typing on a computer keyboard:

Why Your Software Will Die Before Its Time.

Entropy. It's the Grim Reaper of software development. As your code is modified and enhanced over time, its structure gradually breaks down. Until one day it simply can't be maintained anymore—not by you, not by anyone.[1]

The kinds of changes driving today's severe maintenance challenge, as well as their perceived importance, are suggested by the following lead copy from a twelve-page, four-color, glossy advertisement that was pasted into a recent issue of *Computerworld*:

Today, information management professionals face more daunting problems than ever before. The applications you develop must meet business needs that seem to change daily. Mergers and acquisitions create demanding integration scenarios. The introduction of new technology brings with it the need for multiple platform deployment. You're feeling pressure for client/server processing from management and users alike. Meanwhile, the backlog of existing applications you need to maintain and enhance keeps growing.[2]

---

[1] Set Laboratories advertisement in *CASE Trends* 4 (6) September 1992.
[2] KnowledgeWare advertisement, insert, *Computerworld*, November 2, 1992.

As computer systems have become larger, more complex, and more important to the success of enterprises, maintainability has assumed greater and greater importance.

Software systems which are readily maintainable allow the enterprises using them to adapt quickly and smoothly to changes in their environment. Those systems which are not maintainable become a terrible burden, especially if they are essential systems. Accordingly, it has become more and more important for software engineers to build systems that not only work well now, but that also can be evolved without difficulty. In this chapter we examine not the process of software maintenance, but the characteristics of maintainable software systems.

In the preceding chapter we described software development as a social learning process, and held that in an important sense it is the capital goods themselves that learn—the software embodies the knowledge of many contributors, each of whom knows only a little of what the others know. Only in the software itself is all the relevant knowledge to be found. It follows, then, that what it means for software to be maintained—changed, adapted, enhanced—is for it to come to embody more and different knowledge than it embodied before. Our task, therefore, is to look for the characteristics that allow software to embody new knowledge readily. These characteristics can be summed up in a single word: *modularity*. Modularity facilitates the social learning process of software development fundamentally by making the software system more understandable. To continue the figure of speech of software "learning," in this chapter we will investigate the way modularity helps software learn easily by making it understandable to those who must build new knowledge into it.

The term *software maintenance* may seem strange to those unaccustomed to its use in the software field, because software does not wear out and, hence, should need no maintenance. To economists, however, the term makes sense. As Hayek (1935) has stressed, to maintain capital is fundamentally to maintain its *value* in the evolving capital structure. Obsolescence is just as important as wear and tear. In this view, the term is not misapplied. It refers to any activities aimed at keeping software running as needed, from mundane fixing of bugs to adding necessary enhancements.

As the term is used, however, it refers to more than activity that prevents software from losing value; it refers also to additional development of the software that may increase its value. Sam Adams says that software "should be treated as a corporate asset that can *appreciate* through investment in its quality and reusability" (1992b, p. 6). In this work, by software *maintenance,* and related terms *enhancement* and *evolution,* we will mean any changes made to software aimed at maintaining or increasing its value by improving its usefulness in the evolving capital structure. We mean, in short, investment in existing software assets.

Note that we draw no sharp distinction between the activities involved in initial software development and those involved in software maintenance. Indeed, many software developers mislead themselves in seeing these activities as somehow different and separate. Software development seems to be an ongoing learning process, with much the same kinds of activities carried out whether a first version of a product has been shipped or not. The dialog-like process that goes on among various users and designers at early prototyping stages continues in one way or another through "the maintenance stage." At this point, users are reacting not to a prototype, but rather to a delivered version of the product. Nevertheless, the users are still learning from the software, and the designers (maintainers) are still learning from the users what is needed and from the developing product what is possible. There is continuity between initial software development and maintenance. The categorical distinction turns not so much on what the software developers do, but on the legal and contractual issue of whether an agreed-on first version has been shipped or not.

We focus on maintenance for the purposes of this chapter because in maintenance the greater or lesser ease of adaptation appears. But ultimately our attention is on the design process rather than the maintenance process. By looking at software that is hard or easy to maintain, we gain insight into the design characteristics of evolvable software: How do we design software so that it will be maintainable, so that it can be improved over time?

EVOLVABILITY AS A DESIGN GOAL

There is general agreement in the software industry that ease of maintenance is crucial. Practitioners in the software world clearly expect continuous change, although they cannot know just what those changes will be. In economists' terms, they face uncertainty (Knight 1971). They are foresighted, though without a clear vision of the future.[3] Accordingly, they must plan as best they can to meet those changes, whatever they may be. As Hayek says,

> With respect to [changes of technical knowledge or invention] the idea of foresight evidently presents some difficulty, since an invention which has been foreseen in all details would not be an invention. All we can here assume is that people anticipate that the process used now will at some definite date be superseded by some new process not yet known in detail. (1935, p. 97)

It appears that software developers have not always anticipated that change would come as soon as it generally does. As we have seen, in earlier days many software developers seem to have overlooked the pervasiveness of change and tried to build software to specifications they assumed to be fixed. But the years and budget overruns have made the lesson painfully clear: change never ceases. Indeed, it seems to accelerate. Accordingly, the best developers now try to build software so as to facilitate change in general. Good design, in an uncertain world, is design which prepares for change. A major goal of good software design, then, is to ensure design *evolvability*.

COEVOLUTIONARY DEVELOPMENT

The evolution of complex systems, such as the capital structure, is not a movement toward some particular endpoint, or even in some

---

[3]Lachmann writes:

> [T]he purpose of all capital, hence also of the current maintenance of existing capital goods, is to secure a future income stream. But the future is unknowable, though not unimaginable, and men have to use knowledge substitutes in order to evaluate future income streams, viz. expectations. (1975, p. 2)

particular direction. Evolution is necessarily *coevolution* of the different elements of the system. In the capital structure, this means that which tools become useful and which become obsolete at any time is determined by what *other* tools happen to be developed also, and what other technologies happen to be discovered.[4]

Consequently "the best solution" to a particular problem is a mirage that appears when one focuses on the moment. In another moment the problem will have changed, and there will be a new "best solution," for the simple reason that others have been working on related problems. There is no fixed skeleton or underlying architecture for the capital structure. The skeleton—the architecture—grows organically as particular entrepreneurs make particular choices. (Indeed, it is more helpful to think of the capital structure [and the economy in general] not as a *structure* at all, but rather an ecosystem. The notion of structure is too static. Ecosystem captures better the interdependence and ceaseless mutual adjustments of the different elements.)[5] Each choice in response to a particular aspect of a problem poses a new, or at least a changed, problem for other participants in the process. In the words of Peter Allen, a specialist on evolutionary dynamics at the International Ecotechnology Research Centre:

> Evolution is not just about the solving of optimization problems, but also about the optimization problems *posed* to other populations. It is the emergence of selfconsistent "sets" of populations, both posing and solving the problems and opportunities of their mutual existence that characterizes evolutionary dynamics. (1990, p. 25)

Software developers, then, must try to build their products so that they can readily evolve to maintain a reasonably good fit in the evolving capital structure around them, regardless of how—out of a broad continuum of possibilities—that capital structure may evolve.

4Other factors include people's expectations, the interest rate, availability of skilled personnel, and so on. See Lachmann (1986) and Hayek (1935).

5For a fascinating and readable discussion of this point of view, see *Bionomics* by Michael Rothschild.

THE OPTIMIZATION TRAP

Crucially, this means that *optimization* of software for any task, *as defined at a particular moment,* should usually be sacrificed for greater flexibility of design. This is not to say that achieving an excellent fit between software and given task should be ignored; of course suitability to a particular set of specifications is important. But hard experience has shown optimization as such to be highly problematical, because optimization trades off against flexibility. As Bertrand Meyer puts it, in discussing tradeoffs among different goals of software design,

> . . . optimal efficiency would require perfect adaptation to a particular hardware and software environment, which is the opposite of portability, and perfect adaptation to a particular specification, whereas extendibility and reusability[6] push towards solving problems more general than the one initially given. (1988, p.7)

Software designs, in today's business environment, are like organisms in an ever-changing ecosystem: if they cannot mutate with reasonable ease, the species is likely to disappear. In this we find an illustration of a basic principle of evolution. In Peter Allen's words,

> . . . evolution does not lead to individuals with optimal behavior, but to diverse populations with the resulting *ability to learn.* The real world is not only about efficient performance but also the capacity to adapt. What is found is that *variability* at the microscopic level, individual diversity, is part of evolutionary strategy. . . In other words, in the shifting landscape of a world in continuous evolution, the *ability to climb*[7] is perhaps what counts, and what we see as a result of evolution are not popu-

---

[6]We discuss extendibility and reusability below.

[7]"Climbing" here refers to "hill-climbing," a metaphorical term in ecology referring to the ability of a species to develop characteristics that enable it to flourish—to climb the "hill," defined in characteristic-space, of characteristics suited to survival in a given configuration of populations and resources.

lations with "optimal behavior" at each instant, but rather
actors that can learn! (1990, p. 15)

In other words, to be successful over time, the entities that
populate complex, dynamic systems—whether species in the natural world or software systems in the capital structure—must not be
optimized for a certain set of conditions, but *evolved for evolvability*. In the software setting, the "actors" are software product versions and lines, which compete in the economy for wider use. A
product perfectly adapted for, say, an IBM mainframe system
using identical terminals all at one site is likely to be in trouble
when the company using it decides to downsize to a network of
various workstations and PCs, communicating over a network
spread across five cities. That species of software would be much
more survivable were it less optimized and more evolvable.

ASPECTS OF SOFTWARE EVOLVABILITY

There are two main kinds of software evolvability for us to consider. In Bertrand Meyer's terminology, these are as follows:

- *extendibility*—the ease with which software products may be
  adapted to changes of specifications, and

- *compatibility*—the ease with which software products may be
  combined with others (1988, pp. 5–6).

It is important to remember that all software, except for very
simple, short programs, comprises *systems* of related functionality.
To maintain awareness of the complexity of software, it is helpful
to think of it as being more like a factory, embodying a variety of
machines and processes all working together, than like a single
machine. From this perspective, software extendibility is a matter
of what economist Ludwig Lachmann calls *capital recombination*. In
adapting software to changes in the specifications, some elements
of its functionality are eliminated, some replaced, and others
added in much the same way that some machines or processes are
eliminated, replaced, or added in retooling a factory to new production demands. Software extendibility is the ease with which
these changes can be made.

Similarly, software compatibility is matter of capital *complementarity*. A software application or component is compatible with others when it will work with them. It is incompatible when it is so highly specialized for some particular original purpose or context that it cannot easily be made to work with the others.

It is important to remember that our attention here, as throughout this work, is on designs, rather than on particular instances of designs. For instance, we are concerned with how hard or easy it is for Microsoft to evolve the design of Word for Windows—enhancing it or enabling it to work smoothly with some other programs—not with how hard or easy it is to change the copy I use to write these words. Similarly, in applying the lessons we learn here to "hard" tools, we are concerned, say, with how easily a locomotive manufacturer may design the next generation of locomotive, not with how easily some railroad company may rebuild a particular locomotive to achieve higher levels of performance.

The challenge of software maintenance, with its corresponding imperative that software be evolvable, casts an interesting light on Austrian economists' work on capital maintenance and capital evolution. Both Hayek and Lachmann discuss the necessity for producers to restructure their capital combinations when inevitable changes occur. Neither, however, emphasizes the issue raised here, of maintaining flexibility in the capital structure so as to be able to cope with future changes that cannot be fully anticipated. Lachmann, for example, in *Capital and Its Structure* speaks of "the changing pattern of resource use which the divergence of results actually experienced from what they had been expected to be, imposes on entrepreneurs" (1978, p. 35). Similarly, in "Another Look at the Theory of Capital" he says,

> The capital stock in existence always contains "fossils", items that will not be replaced and would not exist at all had their future fate been correctly foreseen at the date of their investment. (1986, p. 61)

Focusing as he does on changes that must be made in the capital structure when entrepreneurs incorrectly forecast the future, Lachmann seems to suggest that entrepreneurs commit themselves rather firmly to their vision of the future, tying their capital investments tightly to the future needs they anticipate, and allowing themselves little flexibility to adjust if events take a different path. In such cases we can properly speak, as Lachmann does, of "failure" and "error."

The efforts that software developers make to build software that is evolvable suggests the slightly different view that successful producers of capital goods do not commit themselves so completely to a particular view of the future. In order to maintain evolvability of their designs, especially in our time of astonishingly rapid capital structure evolution, producers of capital goods must not commit themselves to a particular view of the future, but rather make their best estimate of a range of likely paths of capital structure evolution, and build into the design of their products the flexibility with which to cope with this range of paths. The upshot is very much the same, of course: there must be constant adjustment because the future was not, and could not be, correctly anticipated in all its detail. But many of the imperfectly adapted capital goods in use at any time can be seen as imperfect not as a result of failure, but as a result of planned flexibility. Recall Peter Allen's comments quoted above that "what we see as a result of evolution are not populations with 'optimal behavior' at each instant, but rather actors that can learn!"

EVOLVABILITY THROUGH MODULARITY

It is generally accepted in software engineering that modularity is crucial to software extendibility, compatibility, and also reusability, which we take up below. Why? How does modularity facilitate evolution? What aspects of modularity are important, and how are they related to characteristics of the social learning process? These are the questions we take up in this section.

HOW MODULARITY PROMOTES EVOLVABILITY

Simply stated, modularity leads to evolvability for two related reasons: 1) it reduces the amount of change necessary, and 2) it makes what must be changed more obvious. The first point seems to be well appreciated in software engineering circles, but the second is far more important. In order for a software system to evolve smoothly as its users and builders learn how it could be better, its overall structure must allow the system engineers to change it without too much difficulty. The enhancements can be addition of new capabilities, replacement of some part of the system's functionality with better, substantial redesign of the system, or some combination of these. When software architecture is appropriately modular, with functionality encapsulated in relatively independent modules, making the necessary changes is relatively easy. This is because changes are confined to few modules, and therefore fairly easy to identify. In non-modular architectures, by contrast, there are many interdependencies among different parts of the system. This makes the adaptation or extension very hard to accomplish, because so many different parts of the system are affected that it is not clear what must be done.

The *amount* of work involved is not the main issue; the issue is *understanding* what work must be done. True, where there are many interdependencies among different parts of the systems (we don't call them modules because the existence of many interdependencies implies that the system is *not* modular), there will be more work to do restoring the system's integrity when a change is made. But a far more important problem than the sheer volume of recoding is the danger that what recoding must be changed will not be clear. A non-modular system will be significantly more difficult to understand than a modular one. Accordingly, when functionality is added or changed, or when restructuring is necessary, it is less clear what parts of the non-modular system are affected, and much more effort must be expended finding out where problems remain. Here again is the complexity constraint we mentioned in Chapter 2. Software development is a learning process: *if a system cannot be understood, then further learning in respect to it is hindered.* In extreme cases of multiple interdependencies in large systems, the system becomes literally incomprehensible, and adding or changing functionality in any but trivial ways is so difficult that the task is not one of change, but of recreating the system entirely. That particular software species, so to speak, becomes extinct, because it can no longer adapt to the changing climate of business.

Modularity makes possible the evolution of extremely complex systems because it allows people to understand the system in pieces at various levels of abstraction. Each module is understandable as an entity on its own, and the overall system structure is understandable in terms of the relationships among these entities. Although no one can understand a whole system in its entirety all at once, in order to maintain the system it is necessary only to understand clearly defined pieces of the whole and their interrelationships with near neighbors.

An important factor here is the limitation on what participants in the development process need to know. This is called information hiding. We take it up in more detail below. Information hiding facilitates division of knowledge in the development process by making it unnecessary for a programmer working on one module to know very much about another module. Generally speaking, all one needs to know is what services a module provides and how to ask for those services. *How* those services are provided is irrelevant.

Finally, appropriate modularity promotes evolvability because it leads to decentralized rather than hierarchical architectures, making it easier to add functionality. Traditional design approaches frequently involve functional decomposition, in which a central function or purpose for the system is systematically broken down into subprocesses at ever more refined levels. In such architectures, it is difficult to add pieces without reconstructing much of the whole. Modular architectures, by contrast, tend to be designed by representing the various parts of the system being modeled. With such decentralized architectures, the pieces have a more equal relationship; the structure is more organic. Adding functionality is more like adding a node to a network than reconstructing a rigid skeleton.

KINDS OF MODULARITY

What, exactly, do we mean by modularity? What are its aspects? There are several, and they are not all complementary. In fact, designers must often decide among different aspects of modularity when conflicts arise. The following list comes from Bertrand Meyer's well-regarded *Object-Oriented Software Construction*. These are Meyer's criteria for helping evaluate design methods with respect to the modularity they yield (1988, p. 12ff.).

Modular Decomposability

Modular decomposablilty refers to the ability to break down a problem into several subproblems, each of which may be worked on separately. This kind of modularity must be used to take advantage of specialization and the division of knowledge. If different individuals or teams are to be able to work on a problem at the same time, that problem must be decomposable into subproblems.

Modular Composability

Quoting Meyer,

> A method satisfies the criterion of Modular Composability if it favors the production of software elements which may be freely combined with each other to produce new systems, possibly in an environment quite different from the one in which they were initially developed. (1988, p. 13)

Composability is a matter of what economists call "multiple specificity" (as opposed to single specificity), the ability of a capital good to function in (be specific to) more than one context. If we are to take advantage of division of knowledge, then we need to depend on others' contributions, and we would like to enable sharing across time and place through embodiment of knowledge in composable modules. Where modules are composable, it is not necessary to build anew when a new need arises for their functionality. Composability provides economies of scope in design: one design can serve several purposes.

Note that composability may be at odds with decomposability: breaking a problem into finer and finer subproblems may yield modules highly specific to the problem at hand and not generally applicable to other kinds of problems.

Modular Understandability

Can a module be understood on its own by a human reader, or with reference to, at most, one or two related modules? Code is not modularly understandable if it is meaningless except in context. It is modularly understandable if one can perceive what it does even in isolation from other modules. Understandability is a communication and coordination issue, important because software development is a social process. Whenever more than one person works on a software system, or even when a single person works on a system over time, coming back later to code that she wrote some time before, understandability is important, because it reduces the knowledge overhead for each individual who works on it. Consequently, understandability is also a division of knowledge issue. If understanding different modules does not require knowledge of many others at the same time, it is easier for programmers to specialize in particular modules.

Understandability is, of course, essential during maintenance, when programmers other than those who built the code have to work on it. Generally, modules that correspond to identifiable real-world abstractions tend to be more understandable than those that do not.

Modular Continuity

Modular continuity[8] has fundamentally to do with localization of change: small changes in problem specifications require changes in only one or a few modules. In every-day terms, a small change in specifications should require only a small amount of work. An illustrative counter-example of continuity is the great disturbance caused in many non-modular business software systems when the Post Office switched from the five-digit zipcode to the present nine-digit zipcode. Many software systems did not localize their treatment of zipcodes, and had to be extensively rewritten at great expense.

Continuity is important because the learning process of software development does not stop. What the software must do will change. The more easily these new needs may be accommodated, the better.

---

[8]Meyer takes the term by analogy to continuity of functions in mathematics, in which small changes in variables lead to small changes in results.

Modular Protection

Quoting Meyer again,

> A method satisfies the Modular Protection criterion if it yields architectures in which the effect of an abnormal condition occurring at run-time in a module will remain confined to this module, or at least will propagate to a few neighboring modules only. (1988, p. 17)

Modular protection might at first seem insignificant to the software development process as such, because it concerns run-time problems rather than development problems. But there is an important implication for software development, given that software development is an uncertain, somewhat experimental process. That is, where there is modular protection and errors tend not to spread, programmers feel freer to experiment and hence to discover solutions. Ward Cunningham reports, for example, that in his team's development of the WyCash+ portfolio management package, which is built in Smalltalk with careful attention to modularity, they sometimes attempted major restructuring of the system. Sometimes the attempt would fail and they would have to revert to a previous version, but on other occasions they could accomplish significant change with surprising ease.[9] In contrast, one frequently hears that programmers who work on large programs built with conventional techniques and without the support of object-oriented languages are "terrified to make changes because they are afraid that it [the entire system] will break."[10]

Software development is a learning process, during which the developers learn a great deal from their interaction with their evolving design. Frequently they learn that some prior design decision was flawed in such a way as to make the system less evolvable over time. If developers are afraid to try to improve their designs as they learn, fearing disastrous results, the software will come to

---

[9]Personal interview, October 1992.

[10]This observation was made to me by Bill Waldron of Krautkamer Branson in informal conversation. Krautkamer Branson builds ultrasonic flaw detection devices, using the C language for their software.

embody less knowledge now, and less evolvability for the future. Modular protection thus fosters effective software development in an important way.

DESIGN PRINCIPLES THAT YIELD MODULARITY

We have examined the benefits of modularity in software systems. Now let us turn to the practical matter of how modularity may be achieved. From a slightly broader perspective, this is a matter of asking what kinds of characteristics enable software capital to evolve well. Putting it metaphorically, we are asking what makes software flexible.

Kent Beck has observed that, "when you are in a brittle medium," it is important to do separate analysis and design on any software project before beginning coding, in order to avoid downstream costs and problems.[11] (Such prior analysis and design is often necessary despite the fact that necessary knowledge is often unavailable until users have a chance to see and use a running version. When program development is done in an unforgiving programming language, there may be no alternative.) One of the main downstream costs is the inability to make changes one would wish to make. One designer at IBM observed that C programs often stay unwieldy and difficult to work with, because even when a team perceives some kind of major change they would wish to make to simplify the design, they must nevertheless proceed with their current, inferior design, because to get the program the way they would like it would require too much change.[12] (This designer was working, at the time he made the comment, on a system built in C. He wished to return to Smalltalk, with which he claimed he could be *ten times* as productive).

When one is in a flexible medium, however, it becomes far more possible to let analysis, design, and implementation occur together, without encountering excessive downstream costs and problems. As we saw in the last chapter, keeping analysis, design,

---

[11]Personal interview, October 1992.
[12]Lee Griffin of IBM, personal conversation.

and implementation together in an iterative development method is extremely valuable because of the nature of knowledge and learning. Because so much knowledge is tacit, it is problematical to try to analyze first. Because developers learn by doing, it is problematical to try to finish designing before implementing. When the medium is flexible enough, it is not so costly to make changes downstream as one learns. In brief, maintenance is easier.

What are the design characteristics that allow software to evolve, that allow new knowledge to be built in smoothly? Again following Meyer, we can identify five, and we quote his statement of the modularity principles in each case (1988, pp. 18–23). Each of these principles is rooted in the social nature of software development. For software to be extended and enhanced, people must understand it and work on it, generally in groups. These principles facilitate that group effort.

LINGUISTIC MODULAR UNITS

"Modules must correspond to syntactic units in the language used."

This principle requires direct mapping of terms in the programming language to design elements (and further, ideally, to real-world entities being modeled in the software system). Sometimes this feature is known as "proximity to the problem space." The terms used in the program refer directly to modules of the system, which represent elements in the problem space. In business programs, for example, there might be modules such as `PurchaseOrder`, `Customer`, and `CreditCardCompany`. In a design which holds to the principle of linguistic modular units, real-world purchase orders would be represented by separate purchase order modules in the software, in which `PurchaseOrder` is a distinct syntactic unit.

The crucial benefit of linguistic modular units is that *they make it easier to think about and understand the elements of software systems.* This is important both in helping individual programmers understand the systems they are working on, and in enriching the dialogue among designers, users, and programmers, who can use the same terminology in describing the system from their different points of view. Kent Beck has recently written that "The cost of a piece of code over its many-year life is dominated by how well it communicates to others. If it is easy to understand, it will cost your company less while bringing the same benefits" (Beck, 1995, p. 20).

To see the value of this principle, consider that in older programming languages modules frequently were not identified linguistically within the programming language. They might stretch, say, from line 450 to line 755, and be accessed by a statement such as, "GOTO line 450." Needing to remember what happens in the module obstructs programmers' progress, it is much easier to work with a statement such as "PurchaseOrder new initialize."

In respect to communication between technical and nontechnical people, linguistic modular units make it easier for non-programmers to participate in the dialogue. If the creation of a purchase order is handled by lines 450 to 755, the programmer is likely to think in terms of that chunk of code rather than the concept "purchase order." The client, however, will know nothing of lines 450 to 755 as such; he will be thinking instead of actual purchase orders. Hence they have a communication problem. On the other hand, when they both can speak of "purchase order," the one thinking of the module in the code, and the other thinking of the physical item represented by it, communication is greatly facilitated.

FEW INTERFACES

"Every module should communicate with as few others as possible."

The more interconnections there are between modules, the more likely it is that change in one will require changes in others. When many modules have to be changed, there is more likelihood that the people who have to change them will lose track of all that needs to be done. Thus, for the sake of continuity, the number of interfaces should be restricted. *Restricting the number of interfaces helps maintain the division of knowledge,* because those responsible for interacting modules must coordinate when changes are made. If only a few modules interact, then there is less coordination overhead, less propagation of change.

Having numerous interfaces, with their associated rigidities, is a common consequence of centralized designs. Generally speaking, in centralized, top-down structures, most of the modules at the periphery need to communicate in some fashion with the modules at the core, which are responsible for reconciling their interactions. The Soviet-type economy comes to mind. The difficulty is that everything depends on proper operation at the center, and if a problem occurs there or some change becomes necessary, all are affected. Furthermore, centralized structures imply some fundamental, overarching purpose.

By contrast, there are

> . . . more "libertarian" structures, [in which] every module just "talks to" its two immediate neighbors, but there is no central authority. Such a style of design is a little surprising at first since it does not conform to the traditional model of functional, top-down design. But it may be used to obtain interesting, robust architectures; this is the kind of structure that object-oriented techniques tend to yield. (Meyer 1988, p. 47)

In such structures, dependencies are greatly reduced. Additionally, these structures lend themselves to systems in which there is not one clear purpose, but rather a variety of different services that the software may provide its users. As an economy has no central purpose, and therefore functions best according to decentralized interactions among the agents that constitute it, so also many software systems have no central purpose, and therefore are best structured in a decentralized manner. Good examples of such systems are the increasingly popular "enterprise models." These are essentially software representations of an entire enterprise. The modules represent, say, different divisions of a business or different processes that occur within them, and the interfaces among modules represent the interactions among related parts of the business.

SMALL INTERFACES (WEAK COUPLING)

"If any two modules communicate at all, they should exchange as little information as possible."

Meyer's statement of this principle is perhaps overstated. The point of this principle, as of the preceding, is to reduce dependencies, rather than to reduce communication. The difficulty this principle seeks to avoid is having modules depend on a large amount of shared information—more than what they actually need to interact usefully. *Small interfaces also foster the division of knowledge.*

There are a number of difficulties with extensive dependencies. One is that modules become "tightly coupled" when they depend on one another or on some shared data source. Such tight couplings diminish the division of knowledge and hence evolvability, because when some part of that detail or data changes, all affected modules must be rewritten, and when errors occur, they propagate widely. Furthermore, when one module has access to much of the detail of another module, there is the danger of interference. What this means in practice is that in the development process, programmers will be tempted to use too much of the available, detailed information about other modules in the design of their own, or even use it inadvertently, without being aware that they are doing so. The danger is no less for experienced programmers than for inexperienced, because the experts might be additionally tempted to "make clever use" of some of that information, which may later change. Simply put, this principle holds that modules should be as independent as possible.

Object-oriented techniques, as we have said, address this issue by the equivalent of property rights to data (Miller and Drexler 1988), achieved through encapsulation of data and message passing. No object may directly access another object's data. That is private and contained within the object. Instead, one object gains the services of another through passing a message. The message contains only the data needed by the service-providing object, and the response contains only the data specifically asked for by the client object.

Objects communicate what they have and what they can offer; what they pointedly do not communicate are any details of how they work. For this reason they are known as "abstract data types."

> Using abstract data type descriptions, we do not care (we refuse to care) about what a data structure *is;* what matters is what it *has*—what it can offer to other software elements. . . .
> [T]o preserve each module's integrity in an environment of

constant change, every system component must mind its own business. (Meyer 1988, p. 54)

Restricting the amount of information that passes across an interface is an aspect of information hiding, an important element of modular programming, which we take up in more detail below.

EXPLICIT INTERFACES

"Whenever two modules A and B communicate, this must be obvious from the text of A or B or both."

The reason for this principle is clear: for people to work with modules effectively, it must be clear what they do, and where interdependencies lie. Few problems so hinder smooth evolution of a system as hidden interactions that cause unexpected effects. Ideally, the communication between modules should be obvious from the text of both. *Explicit interfaces help developers understand the relationships among system modules.*

INFORMATION HIDING

"All information about a module should be private to the module unless it is specifically declared public."

Information hiding dramatically reduces the complexity that programmers face and the cognitive demands on them. In a manner suggested by our discussion of small interfaces above, it allows programmers to ignore the contents and functioning of modules they call on. Programmers are thereby freed to think simply about what services those modules provide. Hence *information hiding allows software developers to understand the system better by viewing it at a high level of abstraction.* While information hiding tends to decrease the likelihood that a programmer might improperly try to change another module,

> the purpose of information hiding is abstraction, not protection. We do not necessarily wish to prevent client programmers from accessing secret class elements, but rather to *relieve* them from having to do so. In a software project, programmers are faced with too much information, and need abstrac-

tion facilities to concentrate on the essentials. Information hiding makes this possible by separating function from implementation, and should be viewed by client programmers as help rather than hindrance. (Meyer 1988, p. 204)

Separation of interface and implementation is the essence of information hiding. The interface—the messages or routines through which a module interacts with others—must of course be publicly known. But its implementation, the methods it uses to carry out its tasks and the data structures it draws on, should be private. Others should not need to know them. An important benefit is that when a module's implementation changes, other modules are not affected. As long as the object in question responds to the same message, other objects calling on it for services are not affected.

In object-oriented languages, one way in which information hiding is accomplished is through the combination of polymorphism and dynamic binding. Wide varieties of related objects may be called on polymorphically, that is, with the same interface that addresses some abstraction they share. Continuing with our example from Chapter 2, doors, windows, books, and mouths may all be shut. The same term *shut* applies polymorphically (in a variety of forms) to each. Of course there is a different procedure for each variety of shut, corresponding to the different (kinds of) objects, but that procedure may remain hidden from those who write the client code. The right procedure is applied to each through dynamic binding.

The great benefit that polymorphism and dynamic binding provide programmers and programmer teams trying to create software is that the combination allows them to concentrate on the essential abstractions and not get lost in the detail of implementation. They can use their natural faculties for conceptualization and abstraction and apply them directly to the problem they are working on, comfortably removed from the nitty-gritty requirements of the computer.

An illustration of this benefit comes from the recent experience of Texas Instruments in building a new computer-integrated-manufacturing system for manufacture of semiconductors. They built the system to control fabrication machines built by Texas Instruments but at a late point in the development had to extend the system to control also fabrication machines built by a third-party supplier. It was not necessary to build a separate system to control the different machines. They used the same interface for the third-party machines as they used for the TI machines. All they had to tailor to the needs of the third-party machines was the new implementation code.[13]

GENERAL COMMENT ON MODULARITY AND SOCIAL LEARNING

Let us reemphasize a major point. Modularity is not important to the software system itself, considered as a tool in use. To the compiled and running program, the modularity of the design is utterly irrelevant (as long as the system runs correctly); it has nothing to do with size, speed, efficiency of machine resource use, or other technical matters. But to the program as a design that evolves over time, it is all important. Modularity facilitates the process of software evolution. It serves not the computers it runs on, but the people who have to develop the system. A more modular system may not run quite as fast as a non-modular system, and the first version may not be delivered to the customer as fast as if the development team ignores modularity and cobbles the system together as fast as they can. In the long run, however—indeed, in anything but the short run—it is far more important to have a system that can evolve. Scrupulously modular systems are easier for people to understand and work with, and that makes them more evolvable.

Consider the principles we have just surveyed. Each of these principles has to do with facilitating the relationship between people and the code or between people through the code. They all have to do with helping people understand and coordinate. They all are a matter of facilitating the social learning process in the following ways:

---

[13] Experience report presented at OOPSLA 1992 by John McGehee of Texas Instruments.

- Linguistic modular units make it easier to *think about and understand* the elements of software systems.

- Restricting the number of interfaces helps maintain the *division of knowledge.*

- Small interfaces also foster the *division of knowledge.*

- Explicit interfaces help developers *understand* the relationships among system modules.

- Information hiding allows software developers to *understand* the system better by viewing it at a high level of abstraction.

In the ongoing process of software development, system modularity helps people deal with the complexity of the systems they are evolving by making those systems more understandable, and by reducing the amount each person needs to know in order to contribute.

These principles of modular software construction are not easy to achieve and sustain. Because there is always a temptation to hack a quick solution rather than maintain sound modularity, it requires constant thought and work to adhere to these principles as a program evolves. Ward Cunningham says that in order to control complexity, "when you learn something about how you should have done it, you have to change the program to do it the way you should have done it."[14] This is a process he calls *consolidation,* which he likens to paying off the principal of a debt.

Whenever programmers allow a design to become sloppy, as they often do in experimenting with different solutions, it is as if they have borrowed money. The "debt" they owe is the work they will have to do to get the design into clean, evolvable condition again. The sloppy solution itself leads to problems that are typically addressed with other quick fixes that make the design still less evolvable and more brittle. In this way, the interest "compounds," building up the size of the maintenance debt. Eventually (better sooner than later) designers must pay off this debt by cleaning up the sloppiness and restoring the modularity of the system, *if*

---

[14]Personal interview, October 1992.

the system is to remain evolvable.[15] What this kind of continual design polishing accomplishes is an appropriate embodiment of the problem knowledge currently available, in a robust, evolvable design. On that design new knowledge may then be readily built. Referring to his experience as designer of a large financial portfolio management system, Cunningham says that the consolidation process would make

> the organization of the program closer to our current thinking. And once we did that we were *free to advance to our next stage of thinking,* instead of being tied back to thinking in terms of the old program.[16]

Here is the main point of this section again: modularity helps designers understand their designs, and this understanding allows the design to be advanced.

ACCELERATING EVOLUTION THROUGH SOFTWARE REUSE

The implied context of our discussion of evolvability so far in this chapter has been particular software systems. We have considered what it means to be modular, and what design characteristics tend to yield the sort of modularity that promotes evolvability of software systems, taken one at a time. In this section we broaden the perspective to consider an important way in which modularity promotes evolvability of the capital structure more generally: we consider not just single systems, but sets of systems that are able to share modules. We take up the subject of *software reuse,* a subject given a tremendous amount of attention in the industry today.

Software modules, when they adhere closely to the principles we have just discussed, can be reused in variety of contexts. Increasing availability of such reusable modules, frequently

---

[15]Of course, the programming environment itself must be flexible enough to allow such reworking to occur with relative ease. As we saw in the last chapter, pure object-oriented environments are best at providing this kind of flexibility.

[16]Personal interview, October 1992. Emphasis added.

referred to as *software components,* should substantially increase the rate of development of the software capital structure, and improve quality also. Not only does reuse reduce development costs on any particular product, but also it initiates a trend of continually increasing productivity, an upward spiral of capital development and use, as the programmers build on past accomplishments of themselves and others.

In considering reuse, we must think of software maintenance of two kinds. The first is the one we have considered to this point: adapting and enhancing existing software *systems* in response to changing needs. Reusable components contribute significantly to this process, as we shall see. The other is maintenance of the software *components* themselves. Components can, of course, be more or less reusable as they are easier or harder to understand, or require more or less adaptation in a new setting. Maintenance of components, then, is a matter of investing in the components' reusability, by making them clearer, simpler, better documented, more generally applicable, more *modular* according to the principles discussed in the last section.

Software components constitute working capital for programmers, to be used in the construction of the software tools (or tool systems) they build. When they have components available, they need not build those inputs from scratch; rather they take advantage of the prior work of specialists who have built those inputs for them. Components are analogous to the pre-built motors and gears used by a machinist in constructing a new machine, or to the machines themselves used by a factory designer in laying out a new factory.

FREEING PROGRAMMERS TO CREATE

It has long been lamented that programmers too often build from scratch, trivially reproducing functionality that has been developed as well, or better, many times before. Software components, particularly those based on object-oriented technologies, by providing a greater degree of modularity in programming, make reuse more feasible than in the past. With code reuse, what has been accomplished before need not be repeated. It may simply be incorporated, perhaps with slight modification.

Hence the most obvious benefit of software reuse; the savings that come simply from not reproducing what has been done before. This saving of programmer hours would be very significant even if the story ended here. But the programmer time and creativity that would have been spent reproducing may instead be spent creating, pushing outward the frontier of the new and challenging. This more concentrated attention on new problems leads to an increased rate of software development overall, with a corresponding improvement in society's ability to produce the goods people want.

STOCKPILING EXPERTISE

The range and quality of the capital goods available to programmers steadily increase in a reuse environment. In essence, as software systems are developed, and from them reusable components are made generally available, the software capital structure grows directly. As more and more expertise is built into the environment programmers use, and as more and more abstractions are built into reusable components ready-to-hand, programmers may be more effective still. To the extent that these components are shared in an organization or a market, programmers stand on one another's shoulders.

A number of studies suggest the power of reusable components to augment productivity.[17] Sam Adams has reported on a series of products that Knowledge Systems Corporation built for Hewlett-Packard using Smalltalk, beginning with a project called Hierarchical Process Modeling System (HPMS). Adams reports that subsequent projects

> benefited greatly from the components developed during the HPMS project. In addition, several of the components were redesigned during their use in other projects and were then reintegrated into HPMS. As a result, several of the components were refined several times across different projects,

---

[17]See Tirso (1991), Ryan (1991), and Harris (1991).

and became the base for an internal reuse library that has benefited many projects since then. (Adams 1992c, p. 3)

Among the statistics that Knowledge Systems kept during their work for Hewlett-Packard was an estimate of reuse savings. Adams reports that "[t]he savings often exceeded the actual cost of the project, indicating that much more functionality was delivered for the same cost."

Note also the evolutionary cycle of ongoing development that Adams points out. Components designed in the initial project were then improved on being reused in subsequent projects. The new, improved versions were then reincorporated into the first system.

GENERATING ECONOMIES OF SCOPE

Most programming today still occurs within what Meyer calls a *project culture,* in which a specified project "starts at day one with, as its input, some large user's specific need. It ends some months or years later with a solution to that need . . ." (1990, p. 76). When software development organizations move out of the project culture and begin to take advantage of software reuse, they can achieve significant economies of scope.[18]

Component availability simplifies producing *related functionality,* related programs within the same problem domain. Reusable frameworks at a high level of abstraction are especially powerful, for these frameworks can form the basis of a family of related applications.

One kind of high-level reusable framework is an enterprise model. Sam Adams describes enterprise modeling as "the process of developing a software model that encompasses the nature of the business enterprise itself, its behavior, environment, and rules." With enterprise models,

---

[18]Whereas economies of *scale* refer to cost savings that result from producing on large scale, that is, producing very many of the same kind of good at low cost per unit, economies of *scope* refer to cost savings that result from producing a number of products of similar kind, so that the same inputs may be used in them.

a common reusable framework is designed for an entire class of applications. The functioning enterprise model becomes the reusable backbone for various applications across the enterprise, greatly reducing the complexity and redundancy that is so common in today's legacy systems. (1992c, p. 4)

High-level frameworks of this kind can potentially yield tremendous gains. (Of course the gains come at a cost. Finding the appropriate abstractions is challenging. As Sam Adams says, "[t]his level of reuse . . . does not come cheap.") High-level frameworks bring forward the starting point at which programmers begin new projects, and facilitate communication and coordination among both the producers and the users of related software products. As frameworks become more generally used, the economies increase. At present, this kind of reuse is, at best, found within a few firms, but as component markets develop, we may find these kinds of economies stretching across whole industries.

REDUCING WHAT PROGRAMMERS NEED TO KNOW

A consequence of widespread reuse will be programmer specialization and division of knowledge. As available components embody an increasing variety of design and domain knowledge in convenient, ready-to-hand fashion, the software industry will see ever more of the sharing of expertise across time and space that we saw in Chapter 1 to be a hallmark of economic development. Programmers will need to know relatively little about the components they use. In particular, they should need little knowledge of the implementation of established components. Their knowledge and expertise would instead concern the components' behavior—how to use them for various purposes.

For programmers, the availability of a host of excellent components embodying a great variety of functionality means not only that they do not have to rebuild the functionality themselves, but that they do not even *need* to be able to do so. They need not even think about how those components work, but only what they do.

With tools such as these, programmers are freed to contribute their own special talents, insights, and capabilities to the growing body of programming knowledge, without reinventing what has been done well before. Through software capital markets—component markets, whose anticipated advent we take up in the next chapter—they will be able to take advantage of, and contribute to, an extended and extending order of social cooperation (Hayek 1988) among programmers.

IMPROVING CODE DEPENDABILITY

Component use tends to decrease debugging time, as components become more dependable and error-free. As components are repeatedly put to the test in a variety of uses, their capabilities become known, and less debugging time is required. A programmer using code from a well-managed corporate library of reusable components should be able to do so with great confidence, knowing that only proven components are admitted into the library for general use.

The very techniques that make for good modularity also enhance trustworthiness. As we have seen, one of the principles of good object-oriented programming is to keep individual elements simple and easy to comprehend all at once. Another is to use small interfaces. The encapsulation provided by object-oriented languages also contributes to dependability. Although encapsulation does not guarantee the dependability of the encapsulated component, it does improve the likelihood that any problems that arise will be localized and easy to find. These principles, while fostering reusability, contribute to code trustworthiness at the same time.

Present software reuse yields significant benefit to firms that take advantage of it. Component technology in a market setting should yield still greater benefits. Although components are increasingly shared and reused within firms, there is still little reuse across firm boundaries. To economists sensitive to the powers of markets to discover and communicate knowledge, the prospect of component markets is exciting. Reuse within a market setting will yield enormous productivity gains by widely disseminating the most effective technology. This prospect is the subject of the next chapter.

SUMMARY

Rules of thumb for software development organizations that are implied this discussion are few, but important.

- Don't optimize software for a particular environment; generalize and modularize for the sake of your programmers' ability to understand the system, now and in the future.

- Use the best possible object-oriented style, maintaining modularity of design above all.

- Use a pure object-oriented development environment for its inherent flexibility.

- Consolidate the design into clean modular state at regular intervals: don't go too deeply into "debt" with sloppily hacked expedients.

- Invest in reusable components.

Extending the Software Capital Structure

The Promise of Component Markets

Saw the heavens fill with commerce, argosies of magic sails,
Pilots of the purple twilight, dropping down with costly bales
—Tennyson, "Locksley Hall"

Economics has from its origins been concerned with how an extended
order of human interaction comes into existence through a process of
variation, winnowing and sifting far surpassing our vision or our
capacity to design. . . . Modern economics explains how such an
extended order can come into being, and how it itself constitutes an
information-gathering process, able to call up, and to put to use,
widely dispersed information that no central planning agency, let
alone any individual, could know as a whole, possess, or control.
—F. A. Hayek (1988, p. 14)

INTRODUCTION

Where software development is most different from the development of hard tools, where software engineering is farthest behind other engineering disciplines and has the greatest potential to improve, is in its division of knowledge. There is too little. By the standard of other industries, the software industry has astonishingly little specialization and division of knowledge. Yes, increasing software reuse *within* particular firms is boosting their productivity significantly, improving their time to market and the quality, maintainability, and range of products they offer. Yet those productivity gains are only the embryo of the benefits possible from software reuse *across* firms.

Whereas in other industries the various parts and sub-parts and sub-sub-parts of almost every product are built by specialist producers in a very lengthy chain of production—what economists call an *extended structure of production*—in the software industry most developers build most of the elements of their systems for themselves. The extensive division of knowledge and long structure of production in other industries lead to high productivity, reliability, and predictability; the lack of division of knowledge and short structure of production in software lead to the opposite, to "the software crisis." The lack of a healthy division of knowledge is a major problem for the software industry and a minor tragedy for society as a whole, which has so much to gain from more and better software.

The cause of the problem, the root of the software crisis, is the absence of markets for working capital—reusable software components. Because there are no markets for working capital, there is no means through which software specialists can share their expertise by selling their products and no means of keeping them in coordination with one another as they specialize further and further.

To point out the problem is not to condemn or fault the software industry in any way. On the contrary, we should celebrate its accomplishments and gratefully acknowledge the marvelous tools it has put in our hands. But the fact remains that its productivity is a mere fraction of what it might be, if it were to develop a division of knowledge and division of labor comparable to that in other industries. The difference would be stunning. Nothing else could begin to make as much difference. Without markets the "software crisis" will be a permanent feature of the industry. Only with markets, which enable and coordinate an extensive division of knowledge, will the software industry reach its potential.

In order for software component markets to flourish, however, the institutions and attitudes necessary to support them must be developed. We need a significant amount of social learning through which we may develop the institutions and attitudes that will support such markets. What is needed above all is infrastructure for selling software by the use, rather than by the code. The next requirement is industry acceptance of that way of doing busi-

At the same time, standards must be evolved to improve complementarity of different components, and new kinds of channels for marketing and selling software must be developed. All these changes will require large cultural shifts; indeed, the cultural barriers may be the most significant. And of course, all these changes will impact one another. Components, component markets, and the institutions that support them will co-evolve in an extended social learning process.

THE ECONOMIC PARADOX OF SOFTWARE CAPITAL

In order to appreciate the immense disadvantage the software industry faces because it lacks markets for working capital, let us consider an example of the extended structure of production that exists for hard goods, see how that complex structure is coordinated via markets, and then consider the very different state of affairs in the software industry.

INPUT MARKETS AND DIVISION OF KNOWLEDGE: HARD GOODS VERSUS SOFTWARE

Let us take for our example some excerpts from "I, Pencil," a classic article written in 1958 by Leonard Read:

> I, Pencil, simple though I appear to be, merit your wonder and awe, a claim I shall attempt to prove. . . . I have a profound lesson to teach. And I can teach this lesson better than can an automobile or an airplane or a mechanical dishwasher because—well, because I am seemingly so simple.
>
> Simple? Yet, *not a single person on the face of this earth knows how to make me*. This sounds fantastic, doesn't it? Especially when it is realized that there are about one and one-half billion of my kind produced in the U.S.A. each year.
>
> Pick me up and look me over. What do you see? Not much meets the eye—there's some wood, lacquer, the printed labeling, graphite lead, a bit of metal, and an eraser.

Just as you cannot trace your family tree back very far, so is it impossible for me to name and explain all my antecedents. But I would like to suggest enough of them to impress upon you the richness and complexity of my background.

My family tree begins with what in fact is a tree, a cedar of straight grain that grows in Northern California and Oregon. Now contemplate all the saws and trucks and rope and the countless other gear used in harvesting and carting the cedar logs to the railroad siding. Think of all the persons and the numberless skills that went into their fabrication: the mining of ore, the making of steel and its refinement into saws, axes, motors; the growing of hemp and bringing it through all the states to heavy and strong rope; the logging camps with their beds and mess halls, the cookery and the raising of all the foods. Why, untold thousands of persons had a hand in every cup of coffee the loggers drink!

The logs are shipped to a mill in San Leandro, California. Can you imagine the individuals who make flat cars and rails and railroad engines and who construct and install the communication systems incidental thereto? . . .

Consider the millwork in San Leandro. The cedar logs are cut into small, pencil-length slats less than one-fourth of an inch in thickness. These are kiln dried and then tinted . . . The slats are waxed and kiln dried again. How many skills went into the making of the tint and the kilns, into supplying the heat, the light and power, the belts, motors, and all the other things a mill requires? . . .

My "lead" itself—it contains no lead at all—is complex. The graphite is mined in Ceylon. Consider these miners and those who make their many tools and the makers of the paper sacks in which the graphite is shipped and those who make the string that ties the sacks and those who put them aboard ships and those who make the ships . . .

The graphite is mixed with clay from Mississippi in which ammonium hydroxide is used in the refining process. Then wetting agents are added such as sulfonated tallow—animal fats chemically reacted with sulfuric acid. After passing through numerous machines, the mixture finally appears as endless extrusions—as from a sausage grinder—cut to size, dried, and baked for several hours at 1,850 degrees Fahrenheit. To increase their strength and smoothness the leads are then treated with a hot mixture which includes candelilla wax from Mexico, paraffin wax, and hydrogenated natural fats.

My cedar receives six coats of lacquer. Do you know all of the ingredients of lacquer? Who would think that the growers of castor beans and the refiners of castor oil are a part of it? They are. Why, even the processes by which the lacquer is made a beautiful yellow involves the skills of more persons than one can enumerate.[1]

Note all the inputs into pencils identified here: cedar, tint, wax, graphite, clay, sulfonated tallow, candelilla wax, lacquer. Each of these working capital inputs—components—of pencils has its own extensive structure of production and its own working capital inputs. The whole process represents an astonishing division of knowledge and labor, with thousands of different people, tools, and processes contributing.

How is this fantastic system of interacting systems coordinated? By prices and profit-and-loss. As Hayek has elaborated, the price system is a marvelous communication system, constantly generating signals in the form of ever-changing market prices about what is needed and how badly.[2] Market prices, generated by the competitive bids and asking prices of all the different people wanting to buy or sell a particular product (and its substitutes), summarize in convenient form—a number—the knowledge, expectations, and plans of all of those people with regard to that product. When people begin to demand more of some commodity than the current supply can satisfy, they bid up the prices of that commodity, inducing suppliers to try to increase output accordingly. Conversely, when supply increases relative to demand, sellers must offer lower prices to move their stock, or try to improve quality or marketing. The ever-adjusting prices of all

---

[1]Leonard Read, "I, Pencil," *The Freeman*, December, 1958, pp. 32–37.
[2]See his illuminating article, "The Use of Knowledge in Society," 1945.

inputs and outputs are used in the profit-and-loss calculations and projections of business people, helping them decide what to produce and how to produce it.[3] Guided by prices for the various different inputs for different production processes, a host of supplier enterprises specialize in producing those inputs. Timber companies specialize in supplying cedar; mining companies specialize in producing graphite; paint companies specialize in producing lacquer. *Each gets paid for the amount of their product its buyers use;* accordingly each is constantly trying to read its customers' needs, improve old products, develop new ones, and find cheaper methods of production.

Not so with software. There are virtually no such supplier companies in the software industry. With few exceptions, software firms build from scratch, or incorporate components they have built themselves or ordered specially from a sub-contractor. A software development company *cannot* buy the software equivalent of cedar, graphite, and lacquer. They are not available: there is no market for them. The main exceptions to this rule are basic class libraries of general programming functionality, such as those sold with object-oriented programming systems, and slightly more specialized class libraries of general purpose components such as user interface elements and graphics capabilities. There are almost no domain-specific components for sale on the open market.

There is another important difference, even in respect to those components that *are* available on the market. That is, it is almost impossible to buy them one at a time. If you want to be able to use a particular object built by one of the Smalltalk vendors, for example, you must buy the entire Smalltalk class library that contains it. If you want to use a particular user-interface element built by one of the third-party suppliers, you must buy the entire package of user-interface elements with which it is bundled. That is like ask-

---

[3]There is a powerful information-hiding aspect to market prices. Suppliers of a particular input need not know exactly *why* its price has risen or fallen, nor could they possibly, since these changes in prices are due to the buy-or-not-buy decisions of thousands of people in numerous related markets. All they need to know is that this input is, for whatever reason, more or less desired. That information is contained in the upward or downward movement of its price.

ing the pencil manufacturer to buy the paint company's entire line of lacquers in order to get the single yellow one he wants.

In this limited market state for software components, there is little incentive for firms to specialize in producing certain types of inputs, and little price guidance to tell them either what to specialize in or what sub-components it would be economical for them to incorporate. Accordingly, the structure of software production stays short, the division of knowledge stays limited, and the industry's productivity stays low.

ATOMS VERSUS BITS

What is the root of this problem? Why are there such limited markets for the working capital of software development?

The reason is that "whereas tangible goods are made of atoms, electronic goods are made of bits" (Cox 1995, p. 4). Our customary, long-evolved economic institutions for buying and selling atoms—physical, tangible goods—don't work for buying and selling bits. As Brad Cox puts it,

> Since tangible goods abide by conservation of mass, it is hard to replicate and transport them but trivial to buy, sell, and own them. Therefore large commercial enterprises have arisen to provide them. These enterprises are capable of cooperating across vast differences in space, time, language, and culture to master the vast complexity of even the most mundane of tangible goods. . .

They are capable of cooperating in such a wide network because they have markets and market price signaling to help them maintain coordination.

> The situation with electronic goods is exactly the reverse. Electronic goods can be replicated and transported at the speed of light, but it is hard to buy, sell, and own them.
> *Since bits do not abide by the physical laws upon which economics has been based since antiquity,* the software industry has been unable to mobilize a similar structure of production for . . . subcomponents we call "reusable software."(Cox 1995, p. 4, emphasis added)

For markets to provide their precious price-signaling function, payment needs to be made for value received. That means keeping track of value received. With hard goods, the value received—the useful knowledge embodied in the good—is embodied in physical stuff. Every instance of a hard-good design is embodied in physical matter and is therefore easy to keep track of and account for. When the physical matter embodying the design is sold, the buyer makes the payment for the design. As we stressed in Chapter 1, the value is in the design itself, the embodied knowledge of how to accomplish some purpose. *Each supplier gets paid for the amount of its product its buyers use.* This is true for every component and sub-component and sub-sub-sub-component through the entire structure of production, right down to the smallest bolt or washer. The washer designer gets paid for every instance used, because it is easy to keep track of the steel in which the washer design is embodied. When I buy a car (an "end-user application") in which dozens of washers of various sizes are used as sub-components of sub-components, the designers of each of the washers get paid for each one, because it is easy to trace the physical steel in which their designs are embodied, and payment accompanies the transfer of the physical washers in each stage of the extended structure of production in which smaller components are assembled into larger.

But with software, the design—the useful knowledge embodied in the good—is *not* embodied in physical stuff. The instances of software designs that we run on our computers are *not* embodied in physical matter that can be traced and accounted for in traditional ways. Instances of software components can be created (and destroyed) by the zillions almost without cost, because their embodiment is transitory; it lasts physically for only a fraction of a second in the circuit configuration of a CPU. Once someone has the code for a software component, she can create as many instances as she wants! Accordingly, *given current means of buying and selling software, each supplier does* not *get paid for the amount of its product its buyers use.* Because we buy and sell code rather than instances, suppliers give their buyers the means of generating any number of additional instances with no further payment. How different this is from, say, a washer. True, the *design* of the washer, its technical specifications, can be copied and transmitted at light speed also, just like a software design. But to *instantiate* it, to create an actual, useful washer object, is very costly, while creating an actual software object is virtually without cost.

This crucial difference is the key to understanding why there are now no robust markets for software components: current market institutions are inadequate. As stated above, for markets to work properly and provide their invaluable signaling function, *payment needs to be made for value received.* The value of a software design, like that of any other type of design, is finally provided to users in the *instances* of its functionality, and we lack the market institutions and infrastructure to account for software instances except on the largest scale.

Accustomed as we are to buying and selling physical things, in the software markets that exist at present we buy and sell (or license) *code.* But the code, being pure design, allows for the creation of unlimited numbers of instances, and it is the instances that matter, that must be accounted for and controlled. We can and do sell large applications to end users, and we account for and control the number of instances of those by licensing arrangements, by metering of the number of copies running on networks, and by copyright law. None of these institutions works perfectly, of course, but they work well enough for large applications.

Those few components that are available on the market (basic class libraries, user-interface objects, graphics objects, and the like) are sold in a similar manner. The code as a whole is what is bought and sold; it usually comes in large packages bundling a lot of functionality rather than as individual items; and it is generally sold at a fairly high price and/or with a runtime license or royalty so that the components vendor gets paid something for each copy of any application that uses them.

These kinds of market institutions for pricing and payment involve costs that are so high as to block commerce in any but the largest, most coarse-grained components. From the standpoint of component vendors, licensing and royalty provisions are difficult to enforce and involve much contracting cost. More important, they are not effective enough. It is too easy for people to copy software and use it without paying. In the absence of better means of making sure that they will be paid for what they produce, software developers simply do not go into the business of producing specialized, fine-grained components. From the standpoint of component users, this arrangement is expensive and troublesome in that they must often buy more than they need and spend time and effort staying in compliance with royalty and licensing provisions.

From the standpoint of economic consequences, one problem is that price signals generated in this process are too coarse-grained: they give no information about the usefulness and demand for particular components in the bundles sold. The larger problem is that relying on licensing, copyright, and royalties tracked by hand becomes prohibitively expensive for finer-grained components. The sheer cost of paperwork and enforcement in accounting for the software equivalents of washers and bolts, ten layers down in a structure of production depending on licensing, would overwhelm the value of the components themselves.

In short, current economic institutions for buying and selling software goods by buying and selling code cannot support robust software component markets. We need different institutions, a different way of doing software business.

NEEDED: MARKETS FOR INSTANCES RATHER THAN FOR CODE

Throughout history, as technologies have changed and opened up new possibilities for commerce, new market institutions and new ways of doing business have been necessary. For example, as the potential to reach global markets opened up with improvements in shipbuilding and navigation in the eighteenth century, commerce was greatly impeded for some time by the risk of shipwreck. Many merchants feared to undertake the risk of trading over long distances for fear of ruin on a single voyage. The development of marine insurance solved the problem. Similarly, the development of the joint stock company greatly improved enterprises' ability to raise capital as the industrial revolution advanced; the invention of commodity futures markets reduced farmers' exposure to price fluctuations as trade in agricultural commodities became internationalized.

Today, extending the structure of software production is blocked by market institutions ill-adapted to the special nature of software. It is feasible to have extensive division of knowledge and labor in the software industry, but achieving it calls for a new approach to buying and selling software components. New economic institutions are required which support buying and selling software *by the instance used,* or, more generally, by the use rather than by the copy.

Such an approach, which is known as invocation-based payment, charge-per-use, pay-per-use, or superdistribution (Mori and Kawahara 1990) has been championed in recent years by Brad Cox (1992, 1995), who has also led a pioneering effort to develop the infrastructure necessary to support this kind of market.[4] Referring to software "bits," Cox asks,

> So why don't we just give them away? After all, bits are just packaging, and it costs nothing to provide them. The real asset is the software utility that they encode. What people want is the right to use the utility encoded in the bits.
>
> So why not just let people acquire the bits freely and base revenue collection on acquisition of use instead? This shift in what it means to buy, sell, and own immediately shifts the ownership issue onto ground where technology can apply. For although computer software is intrinsically unable to monitor its acquisition, it is easily able to monitor its use. Consider the following example:

```
if (query() {      /*is this a paid up customer?*/
    ...            /*deliver requested service*/
    commit();      /*record successful delivery*/
} else {           /*refuse service*/
    ...
}
```

---

[4]See also Miller and Drexler 1988, and Cox's 1996 book, *Superdistribution: Objects as Property on the Electronic Frontier.*

> These query and commit calls rely on communication infra-
> structure that doesn't exist today but that could be provided
> relatively easily. Since this infrastructure deals with money, it
> would have to be sufficiently tamper resistant to be trusted by
> all parties. An infrastructure capable of conveying the usage
> information captured by these query and commit calls to a
> financial institution for billing is "just a matter of engineering"
> and quite within the reach of today's computer industry. (1995,
> pp. 7–8)

Under a charge-per-use system, a meter of some kind[5] in the
underlying operating system would keep track of how much certain software and software components are used, and the user
would be charged accordingly.[6] Some means (there are a number of
alternatives) would have to be settled on for ensuring payment,
which would probably be handled on a monthly or quarterly basis
through a clearing house that would distribute payments to the different vendors. (The statement could detail usage for the customer
in the manner of a telephone bill.)

By providing a technological means of ensuring payment,
charge-per-use eliminates many of the current problems of enforc-
ing contracts by monitoring and by legal procedures. Indeed, in a
charge-per-use system, users would be encouraged to copy their
software freely and distribute it widely. It seems likely that all the
software compatible with such a charge-per-use system would be
made readily available on the Web.

From the standpoint of fostering component markets, charge-
per-use has the great advantage of giving component producers
assurance of payment. Freed from the worry that components they
build will be illegally copied and widely used, with little reward to
themselves, potential producers of components are likely to

---

[5]The details of the infrastructure necessary to such a system are beyond the scope of this
book. What we are concerned with is that it can be built—and I take the word of Brad
Cox, Mark S. Miller, and others for that—and the benefits that would result if it were.

[6]How usage might be defined is an interesting question. Some vendors might charge by
time of use, some by number of uses, and so on. The different methods can coexist.
Presumably market experimentation will reveal which techniques are best attuned to
which circumstances.

become actual producers of components. For the same reason, component producers would feel free to charge only a small fraction of what it cost them to build those components; they would reasonably expect to be paid for their effort incrementally over many uses. This low per-use price of components would in turn mean that prospective users would be willing to incorporate a number of third-party components into their own applications, because doing so would not drive up the per-use cost of their applications too much.

ASPECTS OF COMPONENT MARKET EVOLUTION

Software component markets, if and when they come to be, will almost certainly co-evolve along with substantial changes in the software industry and the software development culture (Lavoie, Baetjer, and Tulloh 1992). These developments constitute social learning in the large: the evolution of a body of shared assumptions and practices.

DEVELOPMENT OF STANDARDS

One of the main obstacles to software component markets is a lack of standards. Even though the different object-oriented programming systems all allow the construction of reusable and potentially sellable components, in most cases these components cannot be integrated without an effort far exceeding what it would take simply to replicate their functionality. A main problem is the incompatibility of objects built in different languages. Objects built in Smalltalk cannot be incorporated into a C++ program. Worse yet, there are incompatibilities among the different class libraries developed for the same language. For example, the same class name might be used in two different libraries for two entirely different classes. Although there are a variety of class libraries to choose from if one uses, say, C++, one has to choose, because the libraries do not work together.

Lack of standardization fragments the potential market for any individual component, thereby reducing further the incentive to develop such components for sale. Hence the lack of charge-per-use capabilities and the lack of standards are mutually reinforcing: there seems little reason to build components to a standard if, in the absence of appropriate market institutions, they cannot be sold profitably, and there seems little reason to develop appropriate market institutions if there are no standardized components to sell in such markets. But the mutual dependency of markets and standards cuts both ways. When and if enough momentum is developed in either of these categories, we are likely to see a mutually reinforcing co-evolution set in. If charge-per-use capabilities are developed and begin to be accepted and used, component developers will have more to gain from producing components to some standard. Similarly, if some standard begins to gain general acceptance, there will be more reason to develop charge-per-use markets in which components built to that standard can be easily bought and sold.

There are some promising developments on this front. IBM is developing what it calls a System Object Model (SOM), which allows objects written in different languages to work together. Not only that, it allows classes of objects from different languages to be subclassed by the users as needed without any knowledge of the original language. Hence, the System Object Model provides a bridge between languages.

Another development comes from the Object Management Group, a consortium set up to establish standards for sharing components across networks. The Object Management Group has already established the Common Object Request Broker (CORBA), a standard for object interaction that is gaining widespread acceptance among some of the largest software vendors.

ParcPlace-Digitalk's component-based software assembly system PARTS (now incorporated into its Visual Smalltalk product) has the capacity to "wrap" objects built in (some) other languages. This allows developers using other languages to make components available as PARTS components. Also, it will allow companies with a large investment already sunk into components built in other languages to transform them into PARTS components, which can then interact freely with other PARTS components.

For any one of these different systems to become established as a standard around which component markets grow, an adequate number of industry participants must embrace it, learning its virtues and defects and how it can accommodate their needs. Importantly, this is a co-evolutionary matter: among the most important things any market participant must learn about an emerging standard is that it seems to be accepted by others.

One would hope that a number of different standards emerge. Different kinds of standards will be appropriate for different purposes. Further, the competition among standards is itself a valuable social learning process. Much can be learned through comparing the advantages and disadvantages of competing standards.

DISTRIBUTION CHANNELS

Software component markets will require new distribution channels. Current software distribution channels, generally expensive and aimed at the mass, end-user market, are ill-suited to components, which require inexpensive channels aimed at developers and sophisticated end users. A small-scale software component that may sell for $80 to each of a thousand potential users nationwide cannot afford $100,000 worth of packaging, marketing, and distribution costs. The industry needs to develop affordable means by which producers can easily distribute their components and users can easily access them.

Fortunately, complementary technologies are being developed. In particular, electronic distribution is becoming increasingly feasible. Components may be easily loaded onto the Internet and downloaded by potential users at very low cost. Online cataloguing of components on the Web can lower the costs of communicating what components are available and what they do. Additionally, current advances in electronic commerce promise to reduce the transaction costs of buying and selling components through electronic payment and maintenance of accounts.

CULTURAL SHIFTS

All of the technology necessary to support charge-per-use software markets exists, or is within current engineering capabilities. The advantages of such markets are arguably great. Why, then, do we not have charge-per-use markets? One important reason is that even though such markets are familiar to our culture—we buy telephone service, electricity, some television, and water by the use—there is resistance to charge-per-use in some parts of the programmers' subculture. Cultural shifts in general are an important aspect of market evolution. Some of those that seem necessary in this case are as follows:

Overcoming resistance to paying per use Regarding charging per the use of software, rather than per the copy, there is the particular difficulty that it reminds some programmers of the "bad old days" of time-sharing, when they were charged for scarce, precious computer time. Those who believe charge-per-use software to be a return to time-sharing need to learn that charging per use will be an additional pricing option, fully compatible with pricing per copy, an option that will not disappear. Those who advocate charge-per-use must propagate their ideas widely, explaining how it can work and what its advantages are.

Teaching object-oriented programming from the first An important cultural shift that would contribute to the prospects for software component markets is a change in the style of teaching in software engineering schools. Commonly, students are taught to approach problems from scratch, devising their own solutions to problems that have been solved by hosts of other students and practitioners before. While this sort of practice has its place, students of software engineering also need to be taught the benefits of software reuse, encouraged to make use of industry-standard components, and trained to make use of the prior work of others. In this respect, the software engineering schools would do well to start their students with object-oriented programming as the current best style of programming, instead of teaching introductory courses with traditional languages and then introducing object-oriented programming as something new and out of the mainstream. Once one has learned traditional approaches to programming, it is more difficult to change to an object-oriented way of thinking. There is no point to teaching students bad habits, and then asking them to unlearn them. As industry moves more and more to object technologies, we can expect this shift to occur.

Overcoming the "not-invented-here" syndrome Whether in the schools of software engineering or in industry practice, programmers need to overcome their disposition to build for themselves rather than incorporate the work of others. In like manner, they need to build their own code with a conscious eye to that code's reuse by others, making it clear, understandable, modular, and well-documented.

Eliminating the single-project mindset One of the most important cultural changes needed is a matter of management and business practice. That is, the single-project mindset must be rejected. Software developers must view what they do as producing not a succession of isolated, independent projects, but a family of related projects with a great deal of common functionality. This will necessitate a change in accounting: the costs of developing reusable assets must be spread over many projects; the practice of budgeting each project in isolation from others must be given up. Along the same lines, software development contracts must not be written as they often are today, with payments for development milestones that take no account of reuse. Managers today, with such specific milestones to meet, are understandably unwilling to permit the development of reusable objects, if doing so puts them over budget on a particular project. High-level management must recognize that developing reusable software assets is an investment in future productivity that deserves their support.

LEARNING THROUGH MARKETS

Extensive component markets, if and when they evolve, will yield benefits that will transform programming practice for the better. The transformation will be profound. Consider the current state of division of knowledge in the software industry: almost everything except the development tools is built internally. In many cases, programmers literally begin with a blank screen. This is equivalent to a building contractor's being asked to build a new house, and beginning by going out to the forest with a chain saw to cut lumber for two-by-fours and roofing shingles, and digging in the ground to mine iron from which to cast the bathroom fixtures. The contractor may use tools bought from elsewhere, but he produces all his materials himself. This picture seems to us absurd and wasteful. But there was a time not long ago when homesteaders did exactly this. Only the development of widespread markets for housing components has made possible our present division of knowledge and labor with their multiple stages of production, and the efficiencies and higher quality that result. The minor tragedy of the software industry is that it remains in this primitive stage of economic development.

Of course, with intra-firm reuse, the picture improves. It roughly parallels a situation in which the building contractor has certain grades of lumber and wrought iron on hand from previous jobs, which can be incorporated into new buildings with little or no adaptation.[7] This is a great advantage. Nevertheless, it falls far short of what can be achieved through extensive specialization and division of knowledge made possible by market relationships, in which two-by-fours, roofing shingles, bathroom fixtures, and the rest of the materials are built by specialists, with the contractor specializing in assembling the parts to specification.

Software component markets offer this kind of extensive specialization. They promise a number of benefits in generating and making good use of the knowledge that exists in the software development community, but which is in large part trapped within particular firms. More important, they promise to elicit a vast amount of additional, latent knowledge that will be forthcoming when there are market structures to support its discovery and

---

[7]Of course the analogy is not perfect. Software products are not perishable, so once you have built a software two-by-four, you always have that item available. The challenges to software reuse have to do with such matters as locating, understanding, adapting, and testing the component, all with enough ease that it is simpler to reuse than to rebuild.

exploitation. Almost undoubtedly, *if* the institutions necessary to support markets in which fine-grained components are developed, there will come a time when the structure of production of software is just as specialized as that of house building, and we will look back on present practice as just as primitive as the house-building practices of the old frontier.

KNOWLEDGE DISSEMINATION

One of the most obvious benefits of component markets is that they will allow a far greater number of software builders to take advantage of any particular body of embodied knowledge that may be offered for sale. Market incentives will encourage component vendors to find those development organizations that need the components they can provide. Marketing and sales departments will spread the word with their usual ingenuity and tenacity, and instead of being stuck within the confines of a single firm, reuse can spread across firms. What has once been accomplished well need not be replicated, not within the firm that accomplished it, nor by any other firm.

Of course there will be trade secrets, and often firms will choose not to release the components they have developed for sale to the general public. But as long as any given kind of functionality is generally needed, there will be an incentive for some independent component supplier to try to produce and market it.

SPECIALIZATION

In considering the benefits of internal reuse in the last chapter, we mentioned that reuse should reduce what programmers need to know, and, in freeing them from reproducing functionality, allow them to devote their attention to developing new functionality. Component markets will allow programmers to specialize more. Some may specialize in building components, some on assembling applications with those components.

This division of knowledge and labor itself improves learning, because specialists are able to develop a more thorough under-

standing of and expertise in their chosen problem areas.[8] One of
the great challenges of writing good object-oriented software is
drawing the best possible abstraction boundaries between the different elements of the system being modeled. It can take a long
time to develop enough familiarity with a particular problem area
to discover how these abstraction boundaries had best be drawn.
Specialization will allow this kind of learning and discovery by
allowing domain specialists to be paid well for their specialized
knowledge. Under present industry conditions, with software
being applied to ever more particular and specialized functions,
this kind of specialization would seem to be a great benefit,
because much of what the programmer needs to concentrate on is
not programming skills as such, but the detailed and changing
needs of the field for which he is writing software.

One kind of knowledge we would expect component specialists
to build into the components they market is a knowledge of what
kinds of customization will be needed for their components, and
how to make that customizing easy for the down-stream programmers who will incorporate the components in specialized applications. Alternatively, there might be some domains which support
customization to spec—small firms producing components of that
kind might do all the customizing themselves by special order.

---

[8]Adam Smith remarked first discussed this phenomenon in *The Wealth of Nations,* Book 1,
Chapter 1:

> Men are much more likely to discover easier and readier methods of attaining any
> object, when the whole attention of their minds is directed towards that single
> object, than when it is dissipated among a great variety of things. But in conse-
> quence of the division of labour, the whole of every man's attention comes natu-
> rally to be directed towards some one very simple object. It is naturally to be
> expected, therefore, that some one or other of those who are employed in each par-
> ticular branch of labour should soon find out easier and readier methods of per-
> forming their own particular work, wherever the nature of it admits of such
> improvement. A great part of the machines made use of in those manufactures in
> which labour is most subdivided, were originally the inventions of common work-
> men, who, being each of them employed in some very simple operation, naturally
> turned their thoughts towards finding out easier and readier methods of perform-
> ing it.

INFORMATION HIDING THROUGH SEPARATING
THE STAGES OF PRODUCTION

In discussing modularity above, we spoke of one of the benefits provided by information hiding: it frees programmers from the need to concern themselves with how an object is implemented, and thereby from introducing any problematic dependencies based on that implementation. They need to know only what the interface is and what services that object provides. With the evolution of increasingly distinct components built to be used in different stages of production, we will have something similar to information hiding but potentially more powerful in improving the quality of software development.

George Bosworth, Vice-President of ParcPlace-Digitalk Inc., points out that at present, virtually all programming is done with the same set of tools.[9] Programmers do the same kinds of things with the same kinds of tools whether they are writing a small algorithm or a large application: they read and write code. In most cases, almost all the code is directly available to them. This, Bosworth suggests, is sometimes a problem. Reuse may happen more naturally when the techniques used to reuse the components differ from those used to build them. Being able to see the code of the components draws attention to how those components were built and away from how they may be used. (Additionally, it makes possible the perilous business of revising and "improving" those components, whether consciously or inadvertently, with the attendant problems of introducing inconsistencies and bugs and violating the expectations of other members of a programming team.)

With this idea in mind, Digitalk (before its merger with ParcPlace Systems) built a product called PARTS, the Parts Assembly and Reuse Tool Set. PARTS offers a platform for truly distinct stages of software production. With PARTS, the user of a particular component does not and cannot see how it is built. Thus the programmer's focus is necessarily on how he or she will use it.

---

[9]Personal interview, November 1991. I am indebted to Mr. Bosworth for this point.

Irrelevant detail is suppressed. The user assembles applications using the PARTS Workbench by linking various components together visually on the screen, occasionally writing a limited amount of code. Digitalk is actively encouraging third-party developers to build a variety of components offering special functionality which will then be available for sale to other users of the PARTS Workbench.

Whether or not Bosworth is correct that programmers should use different tools when they write from when they use components, and regardless of the ultimate success of the kind of visual programming represented by PARTS and other systems like it, it seems clear that with improved modularity and easily reusable components, an important step in the evolution of the software industry will be enabled: the development of new stages of production.

Up until now, one has been able to communicate fairly clearly speaking only of programmers and users. Programmers are those who build software. Users are "end users," the people who make use of the software applications. The limited terminology suggests what is largely true—software applications are built at a single, very complicated stage of production. Or rather, given that the work of translating the finished code into machine language is done by compilers at a separate stage in the process, we may say that applications are built in *two* stages, coding by humans and then compiling by compilers.

But when Bosworth speaks of users he does not mean end users. He means those who will (re)use components in assembling applications (Bosworth 1992). This is programming, although of a different sort than what we are accustomed to. Programming with PARTS mostly involves visual tools rather than coding, and one who programs with PARTS is equipped with a new kind of working capital, ready to hand. Hence in this context we have three kinds of programmers: those who build compilers and programming languages, those who build components, and those who use components to build applications. We might expect that as the trend to component markets and component assembly systems such as PARTS continues, new terms will evolve to capture the distinction.

Of course, this division of software production into stages of production potentially can go on a long way, with small components being built into larger components, and these into still larger components, in an indefinitely long progression. Presumably, we can expect this division of labor and knowledge to be limited only by the extent of the market, and the market will be very large indeed.

MARKET LEARNING

A crucial benefit that component markets will give software is more extensive and detailed market learning. As Hayek (1978) has pointed out, the market process is a discovery procedure through which market participants may learn what is needed and wanted, what is available, and where opportunities lie. Of course all we have discussed to this point assumes a market context. The point is not that component markets will add something different, but that they will extend market processes more deeply into the software development process, and thereby deepen and enrich the learning that can occur.

Obviously market feedback drives software development. The public's desire for certain features in word processing or spreadsheet packages—whether registered through direct praise, complaints, published reviews, or simply changes in market share—directs the subsequent development of applications. The same is true even with large applications built in-house for large firms. The application's users are in effect the customers of that firm's programming team, and the users' satisfaction or dissatisfaction with performance and features will shape what the programmers do next. This iterative sequence—the software maker offering a new release of a product and the public responding to it with market feedback—is another instance of the dialogue-like process we saw occurring with prototyping. It is an important source of knowledge about what is needed and wanted: the knowledge gained can then be embodied into the next release of the capital goods in question.

An especially salutary side benefit of this process is the knowledge generated by the multiple experimentation that occurs with competition. In a competitive environment, different providers try different solutions to a problem, essentially offering them for approval to their customers. The better solutions tend to become widespread. Furthermore, the very variety of attempts is suggestive of what else may be done. Sometimes some aspect of a failed attempt may be successfully used elsewhere. Competition also adds a dimension to the dialogue between providers and customers. Customers have the option of simply leaving the dialogue (what A. O. Hirschman calls exit) by taking their business elsewhere. Of course, taking this option sends a strong signal to providers that they are somehow falling short.

Component markets will make all these kinds of feedback finer grained and more extensive for the software industry, thereby generating more knowledge in the system. Not only will whole applications be judged and commented on, whether directly or through exit, but now the component building blocks will be subject to the same kind of dialogue and discovery. This effect should improve the rate of improvement in the software capital structure at all levels.

Under the invocation-based or charge-per-use system envisioned by Brad Cox, a very direct market learning would be enabled. That is, the underlying system would be able to collect extensive valuable information about the nature of usage. Figuratively speaking, it would allow the market dialogue between vendors and users to be more rich and detailed, so that they may come to understand one another better. This finer-grained market feedback would inform subsequent software development, resulting in lower costs to producers and better quality to users. At present, application providers do not have much information from their users as to what aspects of those applications are most used or most valued. But with a charge-per-use system, application and component developers could gather detailed information of this kind. They would then have a better idea of which components to enhance first, which to de-emphasize, which to improve in performance, and so on. Detailed usage information would make it possible for vendors to customize particular versions to the needs of different customers (somewhat in the manner that telephone companies today offer different packages to users with different levels of use). It would not even be necessary for particular users to know which version of a software application they are using. The vendor could simply monitor their use and customize their packages accordingly.

Privacy issues would arise with this technology, of course, but it seems possible to address these satisfactorily. Some may not want anyone to know how much they use different parts of software applications. Encryption technology exists, however, allowing precise data to be collected, charges made, and royalties paid, without anyone being able to tell who used what. Accordingly, those who wanted privacy could have it. On the other hand, many will probably want the advantages that come from their software suppliers' having good information about their usage.

SUMMARY

The single most important problem the software industry faces today is its lack of markets for working capital—reusable software components. In the absence of such markets, the specialization and division of labor in the industry is extremely limited, with the overall result that industry performance falls far short of what it might be. To address this problem, new market institutions and infrastructure are needed which support selling software by the invocation or use, rather than by the copy of the code itself. Under such institutions, component makers could be confident of being paid for the value of what they produce. They would also be able to find out, through market price signals, what components to produce and how.

For component markets to emerge, a significant amount of coevolutionary change in other areas is necessary. Standards must be evolved to enable disparate objects to work together. Better distribution channels, such as electronic marketplaces, need to be developed and used. To support the emergence of component markets, cultural shifts on the part of programmers and managers are necessary also. They must come to accept widespread reuse, with its implications for sharing one another's work and developing with a series of projects in mind.

Component markets would foster a substantial enriching of the capital structure, with greater specialization, division of knowledge, and resultant embodiment of useful knowledge in software components. Truly separating different stages of software production would also foster specialization and allow those who build applications by combining various components to focus on the problem at hand, unconcerned with how the components they are using were built. Component markets would extend the benefits of market feedback and market learning beyond whole applications to the basic building-block components.

Once component markets have evolved, what might the next major development be? (We would not expect the evolution to stop, of course.) Miller and Drexler (1988) discuss a fascinating possibility. They suggest that through encapsulation, objects give programming the same kinds of benefits that property rights give economies. Why not, then, seek to incorporate more aspects of markets into programming systems? They suggest the further market-oriented development of constructing objects that pay for one another's services in some kind of currency, thereby giving programming the benefits of price information about relative scarcity. Such systems would probably be self-contained at first, with the different objects in a program negotiating with one another in terms of an internal, virtual currency. But with charge-per-use implemented across a network, and with the increasing acceptance of electronic payments on the Internet, there would appear to be no reason why an object on one machine should not be able, eventually, to bid for the services of objects (and other computational resources such as CPU time) on other machines. Such distributed, market-based systems of computation are what Miller and Drexler call "open agoric systems." Their implications, not least for very rapid market-based discovery, are profound indeed.

Summary

Foundations and Implications for the Software Development Industry

> *Not in vain the distance beacons. Forward, forward let us range,*
> *Let the great worlds spin forever down the ringing grooves of change....*
> *Through the shadow of the globe we sweep into the younger day;*
> *Better fifty years of Europe than a cycle of Cathay.*
>
> —Tennyson, "Locksley Hall"

FOUNDATIONS

This book has looked at software development through the eyes of a capital theorist, an economist fascinated by the constant evolution of new and better tools and processes. It asks several questions: What is really happening in software development, at the conceptual level? Why has programming practice evolved as it has? Why are certain kinds of tools and methodologies superior to others? What it will take for the industry to make dramatic improvement?

The lens through which we have looked at software development is the following set of foundational observations and propositions:

- Software is capital.
- All capital goods work in a vast, evolving structure of relationships among themselves.
- Capital goods are embodied knowledge of how to accomplish some kind of production.

145

- The knowledge that new capital goods must embody is dispersed, incomplete, changing, and largely tacit.

- Therefore, the process of developing new capital goods is inevitably a *social learning process*.

That software is capital is straightforward enough. Software is a kind of capital good (as opposed to financial capital). All software is a "means of production": software applications and components are tools or components of tools that help produce things people want.

Capital exists in a vast, evolving structure which we call "the capital structure" or "the structure of production." All capital goods result from lengthy production processes, each of which involves a host of tools, processes, and raw materials and/or intermediate goods. This structure is constantly changing, as people build what they learn into new techniques, technologies, and materials. As the capital structure evolves, it becomes ever more complex, opening up niches for new tools and products, and closing niches for others no longer properly adapted to the changed landscape. Those capital goods producers who would maintain profitability in this evolving landscape must constantly adapt the designs of their tools and processes so as to fit with the changing tools and processes around them.

Capital goods are embodied knowledge of how to accomplish some productive act. They are *essentially* knowledge, knowledge embodied in some medium in which it is handy for use in production. A hammer embodies knowledge of how to drive a nail; a database program embodies knowledge of how to store, sort, and retrieve data.

The embodied knowledge is what is fundamentally important and valuable about any capital good, not its physical medium. It is easy to lose sight of this fact when we look at hard goods: the steel and glass and rubber and fabric of a car, for example, are so tangible and apparent that many come to think that that physical stuff *is* the car. We sometimes forget that what makes that physical stuff a car is the marvelously clever design imprinted on that steel, glass, rubber, and fabric that makes it possible for otherwise inert matter to take us comfortably and dependably from place to place.

With software, it is easier to keep in sight the fundamental importance of the knowledge embodied in the medium, because that medium is often invisible and transitory. We recognize software code as software, whether it be printed out on paper, saved on disk, or loaded and running in a computer's circuits. The design—the fully articulated design represented by the code—is the heart of the matter.

Through the wide dissemination of capital goods, people are able to achieve a remarkably extensive and productive division of labor, or, more precisely, division of *knowledge* across time and space. Through using capital goods produced by others, we are able to make use of the expertise of great numbers of other people, whose knowledge is embodied in those tools and goods and available ready to hand. We need not know what the designers of those goods knew; we can simply use their knowledge, embodied in the capital goods they have produced for us. This division of knowledge allows for the development of a fantastic degree of specialization, and consequent continuing growth in expertise, that propels economic advancement.

Because capital is embodied knowledge, the process of developing new capital goods is a process of embodying the necessary knowledge in the new design. Accordingly, new capital development is a learning process in which the new design "learns," or comes to contain in usable form, the knowledge of how to do what it is supposed to do.

Here is where things get challenging, because the nature of knowledge is such that this learning process is difficult. If knowledge were readily identifiable, accessible, and available—like raw data, for instance—the process of developing new capital goods (in this case, the software development process) would be easy. One could select the needed items from a store of readily available knowledge and combine them appropriately into the new tool design.

But knowledge is not like data. The human knowledge that must be brought together and embodied in a new capital good is dispersed, incomplete, changing, and largely tacit. It is *dispersed* in that many different people possess different bits of knowledge that the new capital good must incorporate. It is *incomplete* in that often we have not figured out all the knowledge we will need to build a product whose general nature and purpose we have in mind. It is *changing* constantly in that we are always learning: those who need the product are learning better what they need, what is possible, and how the conditions in which they will use it are changing; those who are trying to build it are coming to understand better what their customers (think they) need, what design elements will be most suitable, and what tools they themselves might use in crafting the design. And the needed knowledge is often *tacit,* in that many of the people involved cannot express to others what they know. Their knowledge is in their hands or habits or ways of working, and they find it impossible to put that knowledge into words.

Accordingly, the knowledge that must be embodied in any new capital good (other than the simplest and most straightforward, and few software packages are simple and straightforward these days) is not readily available. It must be drawn out, developed, discovered, evolved, in a process of social learning. The implications of this for the software design process are profound. If a software product of any complexity is to do what it is supposed to do, and evolve as it must as the world it works in changes, then the process of developing and maintaining it, the tools used in designing it, and its very design must facilitate this social learning process.

A HISTORY OF COPING WITH INCREASING COMPLEXITY

Software has become dramatically more complex since the earliest days of the industry. Initially, when machines had little processing power and storage space, the most important constraint on programmers was machine resources. Programs had to be kept small and designed to use machine resources as efficiently as possible. The industry was resource constrained.

With the astonishing improvements in computer speed and power over the years, the resource constraint has been relaxed. Consequently, the software industry's ambitions have grown, as developers try to take advantage of these greater resources with more ambitious projects. Bigger projects mean development in large teams whose work must be coordinated. They usually require the integration of a wide variety of functions. And recently, this varied functionality must be built to run in distributed environments.

The result, in brief, is such a degree of complexity in large software projects that, in the words of Mark S. Miller, the key limitation on programmers today is "our sheer ability to understand what it is we are trying to do." Where many people are working on a large, evolving project, the learning process of development is necessarily distributed among people and over time. Maintaining coherence and coordination in this learning process, by helping them to *understand* the evolving product, is challenging.

To meet this challenge, a variety of tool and methodologies has evolved. Most of them can be understood as aids to the learning process in that they help programmers think about, understand, and communicate what they are doing.

One important set of tools is programming languages. Each new, higher-level language allows programmers to pay less attention to the concerns of the computer (such as what value is in what register) and correspondingly more attention to the problems they are trying to solve. They allow programmers to think about what they are doing at a higher level of abstraction, and hence to understand it better. Better programming languages also serve to give programs more structure, and thus more understandability. The move to structured programming languages allowed programmers to understand program flow better; the move to object-oriented programming languages has helped programmers understand better the relationships between program elements. Object-oriented languages are particularly useful in helping fostering the social, interpersonal aspects of software development: they make possible a division of knowledge and understandability that was not possible before, as well as improving communication among the different people working on a project.

Object-oriented languages foster a division of knowledge in software development especially by the *information hiding* that results from *encapsulation* and *message passing*. With the functionality of an object encapsulated within it, a programmer need not pay attention to how that functionality is implemented; she may simply concern herself with what messages the object responds to. Accordingly, to the extent that good encapsulation is maintained, work on a large project may be split up among large teams of programmers, each responsible for distinct functionality.

Working in object-oriented languages makes it easier for developers to understand what they are doing by letting them work at higher levels of abstraction than do traditional languages. *Polymorphism,* the ability to use the same name for different but related actions, allows programmers to think and program in terms of familiar concepts. *Classes* and *inheritance* provide a means of categorizing related concepts in terms of one another and understanding them in terms of their similarities and differences.

Another benefit of object-oriented languages in the social learning process of software development, especially the more pure object-oriented languages such as Smalltalk and Eiffel, is that they allow for code that is closer to natural language. They thereby facilitate communication, and hence understanding, among the different people involved in the development process. Most notably, when object classes and methods are given carefully chosen names from the users' problem domain, developers and users can talk together about the evolving solution with much more ease.

Software development methodologies have evolved in a manner that highlights the importance of facilitating the social learning process. Early methodologies failed because they sought to make the development systematic and predictable, in a manner that ignored the nature of knowledge and the complexity of the social learning process. More recent methodologies are tuned to foster the discovery of this knowledge and to facilitate the social learning process.

The fatal flaw of early development methodologies—archetypically the "waterfall model," in which development proceeds systematically from requirements specification to analysis, design, coding, testing, debugging, and delivery—is that they assume the ready availability of the knowledge that must become the new software. They assume that the users know their requirements and that the problem can be analyzed fully and a comprehensive design developed before a line of code has been written or a user has had a chance to react to the design. They assume that the requirements will be stable.

In fact, users cannot say in much detail what they need. The nature of the problem becomes clear only as developers work on it. Designers discover what design characteristics are needed as code is developed and customers react to the first versions of the product. Requirements change as the surrounding capital structure evolves.

Another problem with traditional development methodologies, and with some of the analysis and design tools used to support them, is that by their nature they often block communication among the different people whose knowledge needs to be incorporated into the evolving software. Sophisticated graphical CASE tools for analysis and design have developed, with which development teams can produce elaborate drawings of their domain analysis and product design. On the basis of the requirements documents, in theory, analysis drawings may be produced; from these, design drawings may be produced; and from these, the code may be produced. While the analysis and design tools provide useful visualizations, a communication problem results from the necessity to translate, at each stage, from requirements documents, to analysis documents, to design documents, to code. There is a "semantic gap" between stages, in which important meaning is often lost. The somewhat arcane analysis and design documents are difficult for users to understand. And frequently too, the code that is written diverges from what is specified in the design drawings, as programmers apply their own special knowledge and experience; hence the drawings lose their relevance and value in helping others understand the evolving product.

In response to these realities, more recent development methodologies have evolved that rely heavily on prototyping, iteration, and object-oriented design.

IMPLICATIONS FOR THE DESIGN PROCESS

Software, like all capital goods, is embodied knowledge, and knowledge is dispersed, incomplete, changing, and often tacit. The nature of the knowledge that becomes software has important implications for the software development process. It means, fundamentally, that the process cannot be one of translating given knowledge into code, but must instead be one of discovering, drawing together, and encoding knowledge that is *not* given.

Because knowledge is dispersed, many people are necessarily involved in a project of any magnitude; therefore the methodologies need to foster effective communication among all those involved.

Because knowledge is often tacit and incomplete, the knowledge that must go into a new piece of software (of any size) is not available at the outset of a design process; therefore the development methodology must promote a kind of conversation or "design dialogue" which draws out from the various participants the important knowledge they have and must contribute, but cannot articulate or did not know they knew. One aspect of this effort is requirements elicitation. Development methodology must recognize that requirements simply cannot be articulated up front. They must be discovered. A less recognized part of this effort concerns the work of the designers themselves. They cannot know at the outset what the best design architecture and elements will be; they cannot know even through exhaustive domain analysis. They necessarily come to understand what the design should look like, and why, as they work with it.

Because knowledge is incomplete and changing (as the world changes and people learn), the design will need to evolve. In the development process, users come to understand better what they need, and developers come to understand better how they can build it effectively; therefore the process must allow for change. It must avoid locking in design decisions, especially early in the process.

In brief, the processes and tools used in software development should be chosen and tuned for facilitating the interpersonal discovery process. They need to help the different participants learn from one another and from the evolving design. They need to help everyone involved understand as well as possible what is being built. And they must help the participants think about the problem being addressed.

For all these purposes, an iterative process using prototyping serves well. Prototyping, then submitting the prototype to users for review, then adjusting the prototype and repeating the process, is a means of effective communication among the different knowledge providers. Developing, trying, and reacting to the prototype is itself a kind of dialogue through which dispersed knowledge is developed and communicated. And the process can be repeated as often as necessary to develop understanding of and agreement about the evolving design.

Effective software development is usefully conceived of as a kind of dialogue, an interactive learning process in which learning grows out of the interplay among those involved, their mutual, repeated reactions and response. There is obviously an interaction between the design team and the users, in which the design team learns better what the users want. There is also an interaction between the design team and their evolving design: in working with it they come to understand better what it can and should be. There is interaction between the users and the prototype: through seeing how the prototype fails to meet or exceeds their expectations, they come to understand better both what they really need (which they were unable to articulate at first) and how the new tool may open up possibilities beyond their earlier imagining.

Because software development is a learning process, it is greatly facilitated by the kinds of design tools and processes that help programmers and designers understand what they are doing. Indeed, many of the tools that contribute most to programmers' productivity can be understood as tools for thought—tools for thinking about and understanding what they are doing. CASE tools for diagramming fit this description: they give developers pictures of the different relationships in the program. The same is true of class and method browsers, inspector windows, and other tools now common to the better object-oriented programming systems: they give programmers multiple views into the systems they are building.

Other valuable tools for supporting the learning process of software development are incremental compiling and detailed, on-screen debuggers such as are provided in Smalltalk. Incremental compiling offers the great benefit of letting programmers experiment with small pieces of their design without the whole system being coherent or operational. This gives programmers more immediate feedback than they could otherwise have. The same is true of high-quality debuggers, which allow programmers to step through processes and find exactly what went wrong. Such debuggers provide both an assurance that mistakes can easily be found (which gives programmers a useful willingness to experiment) and immediate feedback. When programmers do not have to hunt for problems, their flow of thought is not interrupted; hence they can learn, and help their evolving systems "learn," more rapidly.

In an important sense, high-level object-oriented languages are also tools for thought in that they help foster mutual understanding on the part of those involved. The high-level classes and methods in an object-oriented system can and should be named for the real-world entities and processes to which they correspond. The similarity of the resulting code to natural language not only makes the code clearer in general, but also facilitates communication between developers and the non-technical users for whom the system is being designed.

Object-oriented design methodologies, which begin by identifying the high-level objects that will be needed in a system, and gradually elaborate by adding lower-level behavior and sub-objects as the design unfolds, also provide a more "seamless" development process. The same terminology is maintained through analysis, design, and coding, thereby avoiding the "semantic gaps" that occur in more traditional methodologies.

While software development is necessarily a learning process, not everything must be learned from scratch each time. All design processes involve, to a greater or lesser degree, the incorporation of accepted, proven design elements. The use of these standard, customizable inputs—designers' working capital—improves and accelerates the design process by allowing the designers to take advantage of the division of knowledge.

While the software industry is poorer in working capital than most industries, it is gradually accumulating capital. In particular, reusable components—suites of *classes* and *frameworks* of interacting classes—are being developed by various language providers, and, of course, by individual firms with active reuse programs. When available, these classes and frameworks can be plugged into or adapted as necessary to serve in a new design. Another promising addition to programmers' working capital are *design patterns*, general, verbal descriptions of how to approach certain frequently recurring design challenges. The regular use of well-tested classes, frameworks, and design patterns reduces the amount of new learning necessary in a software development project by allowing the incorporation of embodied knowledge.

IMPLICATIONS FOR DESIGN CHARACTERISTICS

All capital goods must function within a capital structure composed of other capital goods and processes. Because people and firms are constantly learning, this capital structure is constantly changing. Accordingly, any capital good design must evolve over time to maintain its fit within the capital structure. Evolvability is thus a fundamentally valuable aspect of good designs.

In software terms, evolvability is *maintainability;* the process of evolving software over time is known as software maintenance. The term, which seems strange from one perspective (how can software wear out?) is really a good one from the economist's standpoint, because what is important to maintain is the *value* of capital, and software maintenance is a matter of maintaining (or enhancing) the value of a software design as the design's environment changes over time.

The capital structure does not evolve in a linear, pre-determined manner. As in an ecosystem, the direction of evolution at any point results from the complex interactions of all the different pieces of the system—operating systems, hardware platforms, networking capabilities, complementary or competitive software systems. As different elements of the system flourish or falter, they change the environment to which all the other elements must adapt. Change is thus fundamentally *coevolutionary*. Accordingly, it is unpredictable.

The unpredictability of capital structure evolution puts a premium on a software design's ability to change in a range of different possible directions. A software system's sheer evolvability as such is a great asset in a changing world. As far as possible, it must be both easily adaptable to changes in specifications and easily combined with other products.

The inevitability of change means there is a danger in optimization. It can be tempting to try to optimize a product for a particular state of affairs so that it takes perfect advantage of every detail of, for example, a particular hardware configuration, network, and database engine. But this kind of optimization is a trap. Before long, new hardware will be needed, the network will be extended or replaced, and new databases will have to be incorporated. If the optimization was too tight, it will be difficult or impossible to adapt the design to its new environment. It is preferable, then, *not* to optimize for a particular state of affairs, but to design for evolvability, so that the design can be kept in step with a changing environment with relative ease.

What makes a design evolvable? The key is *modularity*. The kinds of modularity (as laid out by Bertrand Meyer, 1988, p. 12ff.) are:

- *modular decomposability,* which enables a division of knowledge by allowing a problem to be broken down into several subproblems, each of which may be worked on separately

- *modular composability,* which allows modules to be assembled in different ways for different purposes

- *modular understandability,* which allows a module to be understood by a human observer on its own or with reference to at most one or two related modules

- *modular continuity,* by which small changes in problem specifications require changes in only one or a few modules, and

- *modular protection,* through which an abnormal condition occurring in one module can propagate out to only a few other modules.

Modularity means evolvability for two closely related reasons: 1) it reduces the number of changes necessary when changes must be made, and 2) it makes more understandable what must be changed. The second is more important. If a system is insufficiently understandable, what must be changed will be unclear to those trying to modify or enhance it. Either a tremendous amount of effort must be expended identifying necessary changes—trying to understand the system well enough to work on it—or else the programmers will fear to make changes at all. In either case, evolution of the system is impeded.

Modularity contributes almost nothing to the effectiveness of a running program. Its value lies in what it does for the humans working on the program, not for the program itself. One exception is modular protection, which affects the fault-tolerance of a system, but all the other aspects of modularity described above are largely irrelevant to the performance of the program. The value of modularity lies in the way it makes software systems understandable to those who must build more and more knowledge into the systems over time.

Building software in a modular fashion has an important benefit for software evolvability that goes beyond the evolvability of particular products. Because modularity fosters the construction of reusable components—working capital for software developers—it helps accelerate the evolution of products in general by supporting a division of knowledge in software development. The availability of software components frees programmers from the need to reinvent the wheel, to reproduce functionality that has been produced satisfactorily before. It allows programmer creativity to be devoted to areas where creativity is needed. Reusable components constitute a stockpile of expertise that can be drawn on as needed and accumulated over time. Components generate economies of scope, in that those built for one purpose may be reused for a series of related purposes. The availability of reusable components reduces what programmers need to know, providing a kind of systemic information hiding that allows programmers to specialize in areas where their work is most valuable. And the use of components that have been tried and tested in a variety of settings improves code dependability.

All these benefits of reuse are better understood and more regularly discussed than they are realized in practice. For reuse to become as widespread in the software industry as it is in other industries will require dramatic innovation in the underlying economic institutions of the industry.

IMPLICATIONS FOR THE FUTURE OF THE INDUSTRY

By the standards of other industries, the software industry has astonishingly little specialization and division of knowledge. Whereas in other industries the various parts and sub-parts of almost every product are built by specialist producers in a lengthy structure of production, in the software industry most developers build most of their system's elements themselves. The "software crisis," the relatively low productivity of the software industry, is the consequence.

The cause of the problem is the absence of markets for reusable software components. Such markets would allow software specialists to share their expertise by selling components which embody it and to coordinate with one another as they specialized further by observing the prices, success, and failure of different products in this market.

The reason why there are such limited markets for the working capital of software development is that "whereas tangible goods are made of atoms, electronic goods are made of bits," (Cox 1995, p. 4) and our customary, long-evolved economic institutions for buying and selling "atoms"—physical, tangible goods—don't work for buying and selling bits. It is easy to keep track of physical matter, so it is easy to buy and sell each instance of a design that is embodied in physical matter. The designer can be confident of getting paid because payment is made whenever the physical matter embodying the design is exchanged.

With software the case is entirely different. Instances of software designs can be created and destroyed almost without cost, because their embodiment is transitory; it lasts physically for only a fraction of a second in the configuration of a CPU's circuits. When one has the code for a software component, one can create as many instances as one wants. Nevertheless, under our current institutions, we buy and sell code, and we do not and cannot account for instances of use. Consequently, designers of software functionality *cannot* be confident of getting paid.

Current market institutions are inadequate to support the kinds of markets for software components that the software industry needs. We need new economic institutions which support buying and selling software *by the instance used,* or, more generally, by the *use* rather than by the *copy*. This approach is known as invocation-based payment, charge-per-use, pay-per-use, or superdistribution. It would require a meter in the underlying operating system that would keep track of the usage of different software and components, and an accounting system, probably through a clearinghouse, that would bill customers for their use and distribute payments to the different vendors. Building the infrastructure for such a system is "just a matter of engineering" with current technology.

This kind of market for software components would transform the software industry immeasurably by allowing an extensive division of labor to develop. Such a market would (we hope will) co-evolve with other aspects of the industry. We would expect standards for component interaction to develop, through which components built in different languages or for different platforms could work together. New distribution channels would undoubtedly develop, quite possibly built on the dramatic developments currently underway in Internet commerce. Certain cultural shifts seem inevitable with the development of component markets, too: the notion that software should be "free" must give way, as must the not-invented-here syndrome; object-oriented programming should be taught from the first in colleges and schools; and the single-project mindset must be overcome in the management of software development.

When and if robust markets for software components evolve, the benefits will be dramatic. The specialized knowledge of great numbers of skilled software designers and programmers will be widely disseminated to those who need it. Continually increasing specialization, with consequentially increasing productivity, will follow. More and more stages of production will develop in the software industry, with a healthy systemic information hiding occurring between the stages. Most important, the software industry would receive the benefits of fine-grained market learning through the discovery process of market competition and the detailed information provided by changing market prices for a wide array of software components.

Appendix A
Irrelevance of the Mainstream Theory of Economic Growth

Because evolution of the capital structure is so important to economic development and growth, one might expect to find insight into it in the branch of economics known as the theory of economic growth. But, in fact, growth theory, both the traditional and what is known as "new growth theory," is engaged in a different kind of inquiry. Growth theory, perhaps incredibly to the noneconomist, has very little to say about the development of the new and better tools we ultimately depend on for economic advancement. Notwithstanding the merits this body of work may have for understanding other aspects of economic growth, it has little relevance for the present inquiry.

PROBLEMATIC ASPECTS OF TRADITIONAL GROWTH THEORY

Although neoclassical growth theory refers to capital extensively, it says very little about capital goods as such. In particular, it says almost nothing about the relationships among different kinds of capital goods—the capital structure—nor about how these relationships evolve. In fact, sad to say, mainstream growth theory both ignores the relationships and interdependencies among different capital goods and assumes that the tools we use do *not* change. Mainstream growth theory makes three closely interrelated assumptions that rule out any consideration of improvements to particular kinds of capital goods and to the capital structure overall.

TRADITIONAL GROWTH THEORY IGNORES THE HETEROGENEITY OF CAPITAL

A fundamental problem with the mainstream growth theory is that it treats capital as homogeneous, as if there were no important difference between, say, a set of wrenches and a spell-checker. In growth theory models, the capital of a whole economy is treated as a homogeneous stuff that can be accumulated incrementally as if there were no relationships of complementarity (for example, Windows and DOS) or substitutability (for example, PCs versus Macintoshes). It is accounted for in these mathematical models with a single variable, usually k or c. The "actual saving in a period," we are told, ". . . is equal to the addition to the capital stock."[1] In such models, then, there is no necessity to *fit* a new piece of capital equipment or a new computer program with existing equipment or operating systems or processors; we simply throw it into the pot of existing capital goods. All new capital is equally effective.

One important work in the field spells out the implications of this heterogeneity assumption clearly: the "capital requirement per unit of output [is a] fixed number . . . in the sense that [it does] not change in the course of time" (Solow 1970, p. 9). This way of modeling the economy rules out the universe of possible better tool systems that can produce a "unit of output" with less capital input. Capital is homogeneous not only in time, according to this Nobel Prize winner, but also across time. If it took an electrical impulse running over 983 miles of copper wire and a dozen electro-mechanical switches to make a phone call from Boston to Chicago in 1965, it takes the same now. Don't confuse the model with the development of optical fibers and microwaves.

---

[1]Harrod (1939, p. 18). The standard growth theory model grew from articles by R. F. Harrod and E. Domar, and is accordingly known as the Harrod-Domar model. This approach was elaborated in the 1970s by Robert Solow, who later won the Nobel Prize. The following discussion refers primarily to the work of Harrod and Solow.

This mechanical approach to capital treats it like a multiplier: more capital means a bigger number multiplying the effort of labor. For example, if we have 100 units of capital (K) at time 0, and, say, 5 laborers, then we get 5 x 100 = 500 units of output. Then we take some savings from that output, subtract depreciation, and add it to the 100. Suppose net savings are 3. In period 2 we have 5 x 103 = 515 units of output. Capital is treated in this approach as if it were essentially all of the same kind and quality. Its value is its purchase price; it can be increased only quantitatively, *not* qualitatively—no *better* tools are allowed into the picture. Given fixed input of human effort, getting more output with the same "amount" of capital is not possible.

But capital in the world is not homogeneous, so it is problematic even to talk about a *quantity* of capital in any but the most offhand way—we can't be mathematically precise about it. As Ludwig Lachmann points out, "*capital resources are heterogeneous.* . . . While we may add head to head . . . and acre to acre . . . we cannot add beer barrels to blast furnaces nor trucks to yards of telephone wire" (1978, p. 2).

We note in passing that mainstream growth theory not only fails to differentiate between kinds of capital, it also fails to differentiate even between capital goods and consumption goods! For one early theorist, "No distinction is drawn in this theory between capital goods and consumption goods. In measuring the increment of capital, the two are taken together; the increment consists of total production less total consumption" (Harrod, p. 18). That is, everything not consumed is saved, and all savings are invested in capital goods. For a later theorist, the blurring of capital goods and consumption goods is made even more explicit: "The model economy produces only one composite commodity, which it can either consume currently or accumulate as a stock of capital."[2]

Perhaps there are purposes to be served by modeling production in this way, and in fairness I should say that early work in growth theory was motivated in part by a desire to explain business cycles rather than growth itself. But the investigation this book is

---

[2]Solow (1956, p. 9). Unless otherwise noted, all references to Solow are from this work.

concerned with is how we develop new and better means of producing the things we want; theory that rules out such improvements is not of much use.

TRADITIONAL GROWTH THEORY ASSUMES QUANTIFIABILITY OF CAPITAL

Traditional growth theory also relies on a mathematical treatment of capital: capital appears in the models as a numerical variable in a production function. Such a treatment implies that capital can be meaningfully quantified—measured in some way.

But capital is ultimately unmeasurable, as many economists have pointed out, because there is no suitable unit of measurement available to us. We can't simply count different devices: the office printer, filing cabinet, and water-cooler are not comparable. We can't measure by weight. So any physical measurement is ruled out.

The alternative is to try to measure the *value* of capital, but such attempts are problematical also. If we measure capital goods in terms of what they cost to produce, then we can't account for their present value, even though some goods may have appreciated in value, and some may have become obsolete and worthless. On the other hand, if we try to measure capital goods by looking forward toward what those goods might earn for us, we run into the problem of uncertainty. The future value of a capital item depends on the plans of many different firms and individuals, and these plans may be mutually inconsistent. We may think or hope that a particular software package or machine will have a certain value in the future, but whether or not it does depends on how other people behave.

The point here is not simply that it is technically difficult to quantify the amount or the value of capital, but that the very notion of an "amount of capital" has at best an extremely imprecise meaning. It is imprecise even as an accounting measure within a firm, where plans for the use of different pieces of capital can be kept more or less compatible. But as the level of aggregation increases, the imprecision grows rapidly. "Amount of capital" is at best a useful mental shorthand. Treating it as if it were precise is more likely to confuse than to clarify.

TRADITIONAL GROWTH THEORY ASSUMES A FIXED FUNCTIONAL RELATIONSHIP BETWEEN AGGREGATE CAPITAL AND OUTPUT

The two problems mentioned above—the twin assumptions of homogeneity and quantifiability of capital—are probably consequences of this third: mainstream theorists are determined to represent the relationship between capital and output as a functional relationship. This necessitates treating capital as homogeneous, so that it may be aggregated meaningfully, and as quantifiable (at least in principle), so that this aggregation may be represented by a numerical variable.

Not only is the relationship assumed to be a functional one, however; it is also assumed *not to change*. Nearly all of the mainstream growth theory models assume a "given technology." They allow for no technological change in considering economic growth. The fixed relationship between capital and output is made quite explicit: "the capital/output ratio is . . . constant—this is one of the defining characteristics of a steady state. . ." (Solow p. 33). One eminent model is even contrived so that "technological progress augments labor only" (Solow p. 35). With calm audacity, this model forces the economic relationships to meet the demands of mathematical tractability by assuming that technological progress improves only what human workers can do, not what their machines and devices can do. Increasing advances in productivity per person resulting from new capital goods are ruled out. In such a world there can be no fine new machines with which a company may halve its work force and still produce the same output.[3]

---

[3]This is true unless "the capital stock" as defined can be "constant" in numerical terms even while the *composition* of that capital stock (to use a term Solow does not) changes. Solow suggests such a possibility:

> It should be realized that this reduction of technological progress to the efficiency-unit content of an hour of labour is a metaphor. It need not refer to any change in the intrinsic quality of labour itself. It could in fact be an

The problem with an unchanging production function is that it implies an absence of change in how things are done. But again, the present inquiry is concerned with how we come to develop new tools and methods, which mean new and different ways of producing—a *different* "production function." Further, given the unfathomable complexity of the relationships among productive inputs, it would seem to be straining the metaphor to describe production as a function at all. It seems necessary, instead, to address directly the structural interrelationships among capital goods.

MISSING STRUCTURAL ELEMENTS: COMPLEMENTARITY AND INDIVISIBILITY

Because it assumes that capital is homogeneous and unchanging except in quantity, the mainstream theory does not address fundamentally important *structural* aspects of capital which have been elucidated by the Austrian School, especially Ludwig Lachmann. A realistic view of the process of capital accumulation and its effects must take into account several factors that mainstream growth theory ignores.

The core point is that capital accumulation generally involves what is called a lengthening of the capital structure. We say the capital structure has "lengthened" when more intervening steps are introduced into the production process, with the goal of making production more efficient. To take a simple example, producing mashed potatoes (from boiled potatoes) by hand with a spoon involves a shorter capital structure than producing them with Cuisinart food processor. Both the spoon and the metal blades of

improvement in the design of the typewriter that gives one secretary the strength of 1.04 secretaries after a year has gone by. What matters is this special property that there should be a way of calculating efficiency-units of labour, *dependent on the passage of time but not on the stock of capital,* so that the input-output curve doesn't change at all in that system of measurement. (p. 35)

The passage implies that improvements in capital can occur (e.g., the better typewriter) *independent* of a change "in the stock of capital." Surely this conception presents difficulties in how we measure the stock of capital, and invites the question of why technology which yields a better typewriter design is not "capital-augmenting."

the Cuisinart are made of metal, so we can say, roughly speaking, that what went into making them is the same. But the Cuisinart has also its plastic body, its electric motor, its switches and gearings for various speeds, and other parts. Much more went into making a Cuisinart, in terms of "upstream" capital goods and processes, than went into a simple metal spoon. Hence the capital structure of a Cuisinart is "longer" than that for a spoon. The advantage, of course, is that with the Cuisinart we can mash the potatoes in a jiffy, with no strain to our forearms or discomfort to our hands. (Of course this assumes that we have electrical power of the proper voltage, with all the upstream capital structure of power generation and transmission that that demands.) In like manner, all "lengthening of the capital structure" aims at making production somehow less costly.[4]

The lengthening of the capital structure involves what Lachmann calls a " 'division of capital,' a specialization of individual capital items" (1978, p. 79), which contradicts the mainstream models' assumption that capital is homogeneous. Actual capital accumulation in the real world is not manifested in the addition of more of the same, as the mainstream growth theory assumes. On the contrary, it occurs most often in what we might call a "complexifying" of the capital structure, an increasing intricacy of the pattern(s) of complementarity among increasingly specialized capital goods, born in the ongoing growth and division of knowledge.[5] Capital accumulation "does not take the form of multiplication of existing items, but that of a change in the composition of capital combinations. Some items will not be increased at all while entirely new ones will appear on the stage" (Lachmann 1978, p. 79). The homogeneity assumption of mainstream theory obscures this key fact. As capital is accumulated in the kitchen, to pick up on

---

4If you are thinking, "But a Cuisinart is much more costly than a spoon," remember that it is the cost to you of processing food that is of issue. If you use it enough, the time and effort the Cuisinart saves you in mashing potatoes, chopping carrots, pureeing food for the baby, and so on will more than outweigh the price you paid for it.

5Lachmann, following Hayek (1935), holds that over time there develops "an increasing degree of complexity of the pattern of complementarity displayed by the capital structure" (1975, p. 4).

our example above, we see not more spoons and potato mashers, but new tools such food processors, which depend on electrical power. Mainstream theory confines us to spoons—as many as we can accumulate, to be sure, but spoons only.

In pointing to "capital combinations," Lachmann stresses *complementarity* of capital goods. Generally the items in a new, more complex capital structure have no usefulness at all except in combination with other items, and some combinations are substitutes for others. Accordingly, new capital goods don't simply add to the effective stock of capital, as the mainstream theory assumes; they can in fact multiply it, if there are strong enough complementarities or synergies in use. With complementarities in capital use, new economies of scale become possible or economical. These economies are the consequence not of the size of particular production processes (the sense in which we usually think of scale economies), but of the scope of their interaction. It makes sense to invest in a large-scale, indivisible capital item only in the presence of the necessary complementary capital. Lachmann gives a strong illustration: "The accumulation of capital does not merely provide us with the means to build power stations, it also provides us with enough factories to make them pay and enough coal to make them work" (p. 80). The greater-scale economies possible in the power stations and the factories depend for their economic feasibility on one another. Similarly, it is said that the spreadsheet program drove the explosive sales of personal computers in the last twenty years: the tremendous economies that have been achieved in computer hardware in that time have been achieved through very large-scale production, which itself has been driven by high-volume sales of popular software packages such as spreadsheets. In this way capital accumulation can affect growth in a way that is more exponential than geometric.

Mainstream growth theory, as we have seen, defines the stock of capital in its models as "the sum of past net investments" (Solow 1970, p. 4), implying that new capital is simply added onto old. But because complementarity is fundamental to capital—because capital goods must be used jointly with some specific others—old capital is often destroyed in the process of capital accumulation; that is, its value is destroyed. This is another basic fact of economic life that the mainstream approach ignores. Millions of dollars worth of whaling equipment was destroyed by the advent of the kerosene industry; vast quantities of iron-producing capital was destroyed by the development of the capital goods that produce steel; the spreadsheet and word-processing software that made the PC industry was made obsolete every few months as better came along. In the capital "regrouping" process that Lachmann describes, "some of these capital goods will have to be shifted to other uses while others, which cannot be shifted, may lose their capital character altogether. Thus the accumulation of capital always destroys some capital" (Lachmann 1978, p. 80).

Of course less costly production processes are *different* production processes. In terms of the mainstream models, "the production function" changes as the capital structure evolves. But mainstream theory cannot handle such changes. Increasing returns to scale, for example, in which a given investment in new capital leads to a proportionately greater increase in output, are ruled out of the mainstream approach. Growing economies of scale are not inevitable of course, but they are likely in vigorously growing areas of the economy; they can and do result from capital accumulation as it occurs in practice. In Lachmann's terms,

> We conclude that the accumulation of capital renders possible a higher degree of the division of capital; that capital specialization as a rule takes the form of an increasing number of processing stages and a change in the composition of the raw material flow as well as of the capital combinations at each stage; that the changing pattern of this composition permits the use of new indivisible resources; that these indivisibilities account for increasing returns to capital. . . (1978, pp. 84–85).

The mainstream growth theorists, and even Paul Romer, whose work we take up below, assume a diminishing marginal productivity of capital, that is, that each additional unit of capital (again, as if we had some unit of measurement for capital!) in a production process yields an ever-diminishing addition to the output. This assumption would make perfect sense if the kinds of capital being used did not change, but because they do change, it makes no sense at all, not in considering the economy over time.

Because the relationships among different elements of the capital structure are constantly changing, it is absurd to make a generalization about the marginal productivity of capital. Thinking of the capital structure as a kind of ecology, we can say that in the healthy, booming niches (such as internet technology today—who knows what tomorrow may bring?), the marginal productivity of capital increases, or, more plainly, investing in particular, well-adapted capital items steadily increases yields. But in declining niches, such as 5 1/4-inch floppy disk production, for example, marginal productivity of capital decreases—it may even be sensible to retire some capital elements or abandon the field altogether.

Because the boom in one niche is often related to the decline in another, we can't say for sure what the systemic or aggregate effect on productivity will be for any given investment. We have to put our trust in the market selection process which rewards those investors who build capital where it is needed and bankrupts those who don't.

Again, while one can understand the desire of traditional growth theorists to simplify aspects of real-world activity for convenience in their models, one must be wary of such simplifications as those made regarding capital. Simplifications which misrepresent and obscure do not aid understanding.

SHORTFALLS IN THE "NEW GROWTH THEORY" OF PAUL M. ROMER

In recent years, the theory of economic growth has been developed in what is known as the "new growth theory." A major contributor to this literature is economist Paul M. Romer of Berkeley.[6] Romer brings up some of the issues with which we are concerned in this paper, and shows real insight into their importance.

---

[6]Other important contributions include Lucas (1988) and Arrow (1962). For useful surveys of relevant work, see Diamond (1990), especially the chapters by Dixit and Stiglitz.

VALUABLE ADDITIONAL INSIGHTS. . .

Standard growth theory, as we have seen, treats technology as given and unchanging. Where technological change is considered in these models at all, it is treated as exogenous to the system—the economy—being modeled. That is, technological change is treated as something that just happens, but is given no explanation in the model. (Some readers may find this incredible; I agree.) Recent work, fortunately, is bringing the models more in accordance with our experience. Paul Romer, in particular among mainstream economists, addresses endogenous technological change directly. Indeed, the title of a recent paper of his is "Endogenous Technological Change" (1990). Among the premises of his argument which constitute new directions for growth theory are "that technological change—improvement in the instructions for mixing together raw materials—lies at the heart of economic growth," and "that technological change arises in large part because of intentional actions taken by people who respond to market incentives."

Furthermore, unlike some other economists who allow for endogenous technological change but maintain the assumption that capital is homogeneous, Romer explicitly includes heterogeneity of capital goods. "The unusual feature of the production technology assumed here," Romer says, "is that it disaggregates capital into an infinite number of distinct types of producer durables" (1990, p. S80).

Further still, Romer brings out the link between knowledge and capital, ascribing the variety of capital goods to the different knowledge embodied in capital. He treats "long-run growth" as "driven primarily by the accumulation of knowledge by forward-looking, profit-maximizing agents," with a "focus on knowledge as the basic form of capital" (1986, p. 1003). This knowledge is embodied in capital goods:

> The research sector uses human capital and the existing stock of knowledge to produce new knowledge. Specifically, it produces designs for new producer durables. An intermediate-goods sector uses the designs from the research sector together with forgone output to produce the large number of

producer durables that are available for use in final-goods production at any time. (1990, p. S79)

Additionally, Romer takes seriously increasing returns in production where knowledge is increasing. His 1986 paper, entitled "Increasing Returns and Long-Run Growth," gives a "view of long-run prospects for growth" in which "per capita output can grow without bound, possibly at a rate that is monotonically increasing over time. The rate of investment and the rate of return on capital may increase rather than decrease with increases in the capital stock" (p. 1003).

In this work, then, we have reason to hope for some illumination about the relationship between capital goods and economic development.

... BUT FAILURE TO DEVELOP THE INSIGHTS

These hopes are disappointed, however. Romer seems not so much interested in exploring the implications of his insights as preoccupied with forcing those insights into the Procrustean bed of mathematical tractability. As a result, his treatment of capital and its role in production is still very meager. Indeed, his models themselves take the life out of his introductory discussions.

Although Romer talks of and models technological change, the change he talks about is superficial. It allows only for the addition of new kinds of production goods, not for any evolving, increasingly complex pattern of relationships among them. Consider the production function from the model in his 1990 paper, which treated the output in the economy as a function of human capital, labor, and capital goods. Y here is "final output," H_Y is "human capital devoted to final output," the various capital goods are the indexed values x_i, and the exponents on the right-hand side sum to 1:

[A] simple functional form for output is the following extension of the Cobb-Douglas production function:

$$Y(H_Y, L, x) = H_Y^a L^b \sum_{i=1}^{\infty} x_i^{1-a-b}$$

This production function differs from the usual production function only in its assumption about the degree to which different types of capital goods are substitutes for each other. In the conventional specification, total capital K is implicitly defined as being proportional to the sum of all the different types of capital. This definition implies that all capital goods are perfect substitutes. One additional dollar of capital in the form of a truck has the same effect on the marginal productivity of mainframe computers as an additional dollar's worth of computers. [This equation] expresses output as an additively separable function of all the different types of capital goods so that one additional dollar of trucks has no effect on the marginal productivity of computers. (p. S81)

To treat "output as an additively separable function of all the different types of capital goods" is to treat capital as all but homogeneous again, notwithstanding Romer's efforts to consider "distinct types of producer durables." Defining his production function in this way allows Romer to add additional types of capital goods indefinitely, just as the traditional theorists could add additional amounts of capital indefinitely. In both cases, only the magnitude of the capital term changes, not the form of the function.

Romer's equation does address the problem in traditional models that any and all additions to the capital stock have a diminishing marginal productivity. In Romer's version, there is diminishing marginal productivity only for more units of a given kind of capital good, not for new kinds of goods. Surely this is an improvement. But the exponent for every kind of capital good x_i is the same, implying that all types of capital goods have the same impact on production. The model thus allows for no complementarity or substitutability—no structural relationships—among different types of capital goods. It is as if each type of machine and program in the economy functions in total isolation from all other types, neither amplifying nor diminishing their productive power.

Implicitly, then, in this model different types of capital goods are all of a kind in respect to how they *interact*. To a given capital structure, add buggy whips or microchips, buggy-whip braiders or micro-chip fabricators (for the mainstream theorists, add more units; for Romer, add units of more designs) and the effect on output will be the same. Capital is thus still aggregable and homogeneous for most purposes. Homogeneity of capital is further implied by Romer's construction of the production function with constant returns to scale, meaning that output grows in direct proportion to inputs. Where there are constant returns to scale, truly new and better production processes, which let us produce more with the same amount of input, are ruled out.

Lachmann's point that "[c]omplementarity is of the essence of capital use" (1978, p. 3, emphasis in original) is just as damaging to Romer's actual formulation of his model as it is to the work of the mainstream growth theorists. Romer leaves no room for complementarity, nor its concomitant substitutability (and hence capital destruction). In brief, Romer leaves no room for any of the structural aspects of capital that we have found to be of fundamental importance.

To get a sense of the problem with ignoring structural relationships among capital goods, consider the relationships among three elements of the software capital structure today: WindowBuilder, a set of tools for developing graphical user interfaces, Smalltalk, and COBOL. WindowBuilder is built in Smalltalk, for use with Smalltalk—without Smalltalk present it cannot work. COBOL is arguably being made obsolete by object-oriented languages such as Smalltalk. How are we to make sense of "additive separability" in respect to these three? Not only are Smalltalk and WindowBuilder directly complementary, in the strict sense that one requires the other to be running on the same computer, but WindowBuilder, having been built *in* Smalltalk, could never have come into being *without* Smalltalk. Suppose we "subtract" Smalltalk from the equation, what becomes of WindowBuilder? Then it never was. These are not "additively separable." Furthermore, COBOL is being replaced by Smalltalk in certain cases. Then is the productive power of Smalltalk "added" to that of COBOL, or does it subtract from it?

In this work, we hold structural issues of complementarity and substitutability, as well as dependencies of one design on another, as of WindowBuilder on Smalltalk, to be of fundamental importance. We find no help with these in the new growth theory. Romer says, "An investigation of complementarity as well as of mixtures of types of substitutability is left for future work" (1990, p. S81).

The main question this work seeks to help answer is, "What is the nature of the process by which people learn how to fashion better tools?" Here again, Romer gives little help. Within his broader model of a three-sector economy, he models technological innovation as occurring in a research sector. The research sector draws on available human capital and, making use of the current stock of technological knowledge, produces new technological knowledge in the form of designs for production goods. This new knowledge is then licensed to the production goods sector, which may build the designs into new and better capital equipment in subsequent periods. The new capital equipment is then utilized by the final goods sector to produce consumable output.

His substantive description of the process by which people learn how to fashion better tools is as follows: ". . . research output depends on the amount of human capital devoted to research. It also depends on the stock of knowledge available to a person doing research." After presenting a formal mathematical model, he states that "[w]ith this formal structure, the output of new designs produced by researcher j can be written as a continuous, deterministic function of the inputs applied" (p. S83).

Given our purposes, this is disappointing. Having been urged in the paper to recognize the importance of technological progress, we may naturally ask of it, "what is the *nature* of the process?" If so, we must content ourselves with the answer that technological progress is "a continuous, deterministic function of the inputs applied," those being human capital and the stock of knowledge. It amounts essentially to this: when well-trained researchers are given a lot of good information, they think up new technologies.

The new growth theory thus has little to say about the process by which technological progress occurs. Indeed, it does not seem to be much concerned with what happens to advance human economic well-being. Romer's paper certainly is not; its attention is on requirements for and characteristics of a balanced growth equilibrium that is generated by the model as specified. There is no room for process: there is no uncertainty, no real time, no need for adjustment, no capital destruction. None of the richness of a mutual adjustment process in conditions of uncertainty is to be found here. The manner in which Romer formalizes his discussion takes the richness out of it and leaves it little better than the traditional models for understanding the process of economic development.

Like traditional growth theorists, Romer neglects the structural elements of capital. He chooses to ignore that the growth and division of knowledge leads to a growing complexity of complementary relationships among capital goods. For Romer, introducing new knowledge into production is essentially a research effort, not a coordination challenge. In this book, we take a different view.

Appendix B
Applicability to Hard Tools

We chose, in this inquiry, to focus on software development, because with software the knowledge aspects of capital goods are immediately apparent, and the physical aspects are in the background. This has allowed us to focus on capital goods as embodied knowledge without being distracted either by steel and glass and silicon and ceramics, or by the important challenges of embodying design knowledge in those physical substances. But it is useful to verify that the issues of social learning and system evolvability, which we found to be crucial in software, are also fundamentally important in hard tools. We find that they are. The same issues apply whether we are talking about designing and producing a new word processor or a new hammer. The extent and nature of the parallels is an intriguing subject which we cannot take up here; our task must simply be to establish that parallels exist.

PROTOTYPING AND SOCIAL LEARNING

The key concept we explored in Chapter 3 is that the development of new capital goods is a social learning process. It is a learning process because it is a matter of embodying knowledge, and it is a social process because it calls on the knowledge of a variety of people, which is embodied in a form that is available for shared use. That knowledge is initially dispersed, incomplete, and often tacit. We found proof of this point in the nature of the processes and tools used in initial software development. Chief among these are rapid prototyping and a variety of tools and methodologies for managing the complexity of the design process. Do we see the same kinds of processes and tools used in the development of hard tools? We do. Prototyping is particularly important in manufacturing. Steven Wheelwright and Kim Clark address the development of physical goods in their recent book *Revolutionizing Product Development* (1992). They argue that

> ... prototyping and its role in design-build-test cycles is a core element of development and a major area of opportunity for managements seeking to improve the effectiveness and efficiency of their development process. (p. 260)

They focus in particular on "[i]ncreasing the rate and amount of *learning* that occurs in each cycle" (p. 260, emphasis added).

New, computer-driven devices for the rapid prototyping of physical tools and parts are being employed to great advantage by automakers, aerospace companies, and tooling companies. These devices use such techniques as hardening liquid polymer with an ultraviolet laser. The laser is guided by computer-automated design (CAD) drawings of a series of cross-sections of the tool to be modeled. Layer after layer is deposited as a computer-controlled lift lowers the emerging model into the liquid. Models can be used as the prototypes themselves, or as molds from which the actual prototypes are cast (Chaudry 1992). These new prototyping tools are much faster and less expensive than conventional techniques, providing more rapid and frequent feedback to designers and prospective users.

The purpose of prototyping hard tools is the same as for software: to elicit information from the different people whose (often tacit) knowledge can contribute to the design process.

> Because even simple prototypes can convey substantial amounts of information, they serve as a bridge between individuals and groups with very different backgrounds, experiences, and interests. Thus management can use prototypes to gauge, share, and extend organizational knowledge. (Wheelwright and Clark 1992, p. 274)

As with software prototypes, physical prototypes serve as the vehicle for dialogue through which new knowledge is elicited and understood by the various participants:

> The physical object represented by the prototype becomes the vehicle by which different contributors can focus and articulate their concerns and issues, and reach agreement on the best ways to resolve conflicts and solve problems. (Wheelwright and Clark 1992, p. 273)

The physical nature of the prototype makes it more understandable to those whose knowledge is more tacit than articulate. Communication through interacting with a prototype often succeeds better than communication through symbolic representation: Through rapid prototyping, Alcoa has not only shortened its manufacturing review process substantially, but also has "minimized mistakes caused by misinterpretation of manual drawings and prints and miscommunication of design details" (Chaudry 1992, p. 78).

MODULARITY AND EVOLVABILITY

In Chapter 4 we explored design evolvability through modularity. Not surprisingly, modularity is very important in the design of hard tools also. A concept currently important in the engineering literature is "design for manufacturability" (DFM),[1] in which modularity and component assembly are important. The design for manufacturability literature discusses specific modularity issues closely related to those we saw raised by Bertrand Meyer. Design for manufacturability addresses understandability (regarding, for example, whether a part is symmetrical or not) and the nature of interfaces (ideally they should be simple enough so that parts fit or snap together and assembly tools are not required). Another important issue is standardization, for precisely the same reasons

---

[1] For representative work, see Shina (1991) and Suh (1990). "Knowledge-based, object-oriented" computer-automated design systems and their use in design for manufacturability are discussed in Belzer and Rosenfeld (1987), and Cinquegrana (1990).

it is important in software: standard parts are easier to reuse in different, but similar designs; they are more reliable because they are tested in a variety of uses; they are less expensive to use because they do not need to be tested; and they are more likely to be reused rather than replicated because they become generally known (Kamm 1990).

While the design for manufacturability approach generally stresses the importance of modularity to the manufacturability of particular, single products, Wheelwright and Clark take pains to establish its importance to what they call *producibility* as well. What they mean by producibility is what we have called evolvability. They urge manufacturers to think beyond designing single products, and think instead of "an approach to design that comprehends the product family as a whole" (1992, p. 237).

> Given increasingly fragmented markets and the need to offer specialized products that meet the requirements and demands of increasingly diversified customers, [manufacturers] need the capability to produce a high variety of products at low cost. Moreover, [they] need to be able to respond effectively to shifts in the product mix that occur from time to time in unexpected ways. (1992, p. 237)

In the terms we have been using, any design or family of designs will have to evolve as conditions change, and what changes will occur is uncertain. Therefore it is valuable for the designs to be evolvable. And evolvability, in hardware as well as software, depends on modularity of design. Wheelwright and Clark speak in familiar-sounding terms:

> In the case of our gear design problem, a firm using *modular design* would not design a new automatic rewind system every time it brought out a new version of a particular camera. Instead, the project to develop the platform product would include an effort to develop a new rewinder and a new gear system that designers *would use in several future versions of the product*. Engineers working on the platform would design the rewinder to fit a given space constraint and would *establish*

interfaces (how the parts fit together physically, how control is achieved, how the users interact with the rewinder) *to guide future development efforts.* (1992, p. 239, emphasis added)

The principles we have uncovered with respect to software design, then, seem to be applicable to hardware design.

REFERENCES

Adams, Sam S. 1992a. Software Assets and the CRC Technique. *Hotline on Object-Oriented Technology* 3 (August):4–7.

———. 1992b. Object-Oriented ROI: Extending CRC Across the Lifecycle. *Hotline on Object-Oriented Technology* 3 (September).

———. 1992c. Software Reuse and the Enterprise. *Software Development '92*. Spring proceedings.

Allen, Peter M. 1990. Why the Future Is Not What It Was. Prepared for "Futures," 4 June 1990. Bedford, England: International Ecotechnology Research Center.

Arrow, Kenneth. 1962. The Economic Implications of Learning by Doing. *Review of Economic Studies* 29 (June):155–175.

Barn, Balbir S. 1992. User Interface Development: Our Experience with HP Interface Architect. In *CASE, Current Practice, Future Prospects*, edited by Kathy Spurr and Paul Layzell. Chichester: Wiley.

Beck, Kent. 1995. Clean Code: Pipe Dream or State of Mind? *The Smalltalk Report* 4 (June):20–22.

Belzer, A., and L. Rosenfeld 1987. *Breaking Through the Complexity Barrier*. Cambridge, Mass.: ICAD Publications.

Bennet, C. H. 1985. Fundamental Physical Limits of Computation. *Scientific American* (July):48–56.

Bohm-Bawerk, Eugen von. 1959 [1889]. *Capital and Interest*. 3 vols. Translated by G. D. Huncke and H. F. Sennholz. South Holland, Ill.: Libertarian Press.

Bronowski, J. 1973. *The Ascent of Man*. Boston: Little, Brown, & Co.

Bosworth, George. 1992. Objects, Not Classes, Are the Issue. *Object Magazine* 2 (Nov./Dec.):8.

Brooks, Frederick P., Jr. 1975. *The Mythical Man-Month: Essays on Software Engineering*. Reading, Mass.: Addison-Wesley.

———. 1987. No Silver Bullet: Essence versus Accidents of Software Engineering. *Computer* (April):10–19.

Chaudry, Anil. 1992. From Art to Part. *Computerworld* 9:77–78.

Cinquegrana, D. 1990. *Understanding ICAD Systems*. Cambridge, Mass.: ICAD Publications.

Cox, Brad. 1992. What If There Is a Silver Bullet and the Competition Gets It First? *Journal of Object-Oriented Programming* 5 (June):8–9, 76.

———. 1995. "No Silver Bullet" Reconsidered. *American Programmer* (November):2–8.

———. 1996. *Superdistribution: Objects as Property on the Electronic Frontier.* Reading, Mass.: Addison-Wesley.

Diamond, Peter. 1990. *Growth/Productivity/Unemployment.* Cambridge, Mass.: MIT Press.

Dixit, Avinash. 1990. Growth Theory After Thirty Years. In *Growth/Productivity/Unemployment,* edited by Peter Diamond. Cambridge, Mass.: MIT Press.

Domar, E. 1946. Capital Expansion, Rate of Growth, and Employment. *Econometrica* 14:137–47.

———. 1957. *Essays in the Theory of Economic Growth.* New York: Oxford University Press.

Englebart, Douglas C. 1963. A Conceptual Framework for the Augmentation of Man's Intellect. In *Vistas in Information Handling,* edited by Paul W. Howerton and David C. Weeks. Washington D.C.: Spartan Books

Gadamer, Hans-Georg. 1975. *Philosophical Hermeneutics.* Translated and edited by David E. Linge. Berkeley: University of California Press.

Goldberg, Adele, ed. 1988. *A History of Personal Workstations.* Reading, Mass.: ACM Press.

Harrod, R. F. 1939. An Essay in Dyamic Theory. *Economic Journal* 49:14–33.

Harris, Kim. 1991. Hewlett-Packard Corporate Reuse Program. *Proceedings of the Fourth Annual Workshop on Software Reuse.* Reston, Virginia, Nov. 18–22, 1991.

Hayek, F. A. 1935. The Maintenance of Capital. *Economica* 2(August). Reprinted in *Profits, Interest and Investment.* London: Routledge & Sons. 1939.

———. 1941. *The Pure Theory of Capital.* Chicago: University of Chicago Press.

———. 1945. The Use of Knowledge in Society. In *Individualism and Economic Order.* Chicago: University of Chicago Press. First published in *American Economic Review* 35 (September):519–30.

————. 1948. *Individualism and Economic Order.* Chicago: University of Chicago Press.

————. 1978. *New Studies in Philosophy, Politics, Economics and the History of Ideas.* Chicago: University of Chicago Press.

————. 1979. *The Counter-Revolution of Science.* Indianapolis, Ind.: Liberty Press.

————. 1988. *The Fatal Conceit.* Chicago: University of Chicago Press.

Huberman, Bernardo A. 1988. *The Ecology of Computation.* New York: North-Holland.

Kamm, Lawrence J. 1990. *Designing Cost-Efficient Mechanisms: Minimum Constraint Design, Designing with Commercial Components, and Topics in Design Engineering.* New York: McGraw Hill.

Kara, Daniel A. 1992. CASE and Advanced Software Development on the Macintosh. *CASE Trends* 4 (September).

Kay, Alan. 1992. The Natural History of Objects. In *Happy 25th Anniversary Objects!* New York: SIGS Publications.

Knight, Frank H. 1971 [1921]. *Risk, Uncertainty, and Profit.* Chicago: University of Chicago Press.

Lachmann, L. M. 1975. Reflections on Hayekian Capital Theory. Paper delivered at the Allied Social Science Association meeting in Dallas, Texas, 28–30 December.

————. 1977. Capital, Expectations, and the Market Process. Kansas City, Kan.: Sheed, Andrews, and McMeel.

————. 1978. *Capital and Its Structure.* Kansas City. Kan.: Sheed, Andrews, and McMeel.

————. 1986. *The Market as an Economic Process.* New York: Basil Blackwell.

Langlois, Richard N. 1991. Transaction-Cost Economics in Real Time. *Industrial and Corporate Change* 1 (1): 99–127.

Lavoie, Don. 1985. *National Economic Planning: What is Left?* Cambridge, Mass.: Ballinger.

Lavoie, Don, Howard Baetjer, and William Tulloh. 1991. Coping with Complexity: OOPS and the Economist's Critique of Central Planning, *Hotline on Object-Oriented Technology* 3 (Nov): 6–8.

————. 1993. *Component Software: A Market Perspective on the Coming Revolution in Software Development.* Boston: Patricia Seybold Group.

Leijonhufvud, Axel. 1989. Information Costs and the Division of Labour. *International Social Science Journal* 120 (May): 165–176.

Lucas, Robert E. Jr. 1988. On the Mechanics of Development Planning. *Journal of Monetary Economics* 22(July): 3–42.

McClure, Carma. 1989. *CASE Is Software Automation.* Englewood Cliffs, N.J.: Prentice-Hall.

Menger, Carl. 1981 [1871]. *Principles of Economics.* New York: New York University Press.

Meyer, Bertrand. 1988. *Object-Oriented Software Construction.* Englewood Cliffs, NJ: Prentice-Hall.

———. 1990. The New Culture of Software Development. *Journal of Object-Oriented Programming* 3 (Nov./Dec.):76–79.

———. 1991. From the Bubbles to the Objects, in Evolution versus Revolution: Should Structured Methods Be Objectified? *Object Magazine* 1 (November/December):31.

Miller, Mark S., and K. Eric Drexler. 1988. Markets and Computation: Agoric Open Systems. In *The Ecology of Computation,* edited by B. A Huberman. Amsterdam: North-Holland.

Mises, Ludwig von. 1966 [1949]. *Human Action.* Chicago: Henry Regnery Company.

Moody, Scott, and Lucy Berlis. 1990. When Objects Collide: Experiences with Reusing Multiple Class Hierarchies. *OOPSLA/SCOOP 1990 Proceedings.* New York: ACM.

Mori, Ryoichi, and Masaji Kawahara. 1990. Superdistribution: The Concept and the Architecture. *The Transactions of the IEICE* 73 (July).

Mullin, Mark. 1990. *Rapid Prototyping for Object-Oriented Systems.* Menlo Park, Calif.: Addison-Wesley.

Norman, Ronald J., and Gene Forte. 1992a. Automating the Software Development Process: CASE in the '90s. Communications of the ACM 35(4): 27.

———. 1992b. A Self-Assessment by the Software Engineering Community. Communications of the ACM 35(4):28–36.

———. 1958. Personal Knowledge. Chicago: University of Chicago Press.

Polanyi, Michael. 1964. *The Tacit Dimension.* New York: Doubleday.

Read, Leonard. 1958. I, Pencil, *The Freeman* (December):32–37.

Robinson, Keith. 1992. Putting the SE into CASE, In *CASE, Current Practice, Future Prospects,* edited by Kathy Spurr and Paul Layzell. Chichester: Wiley.

Romer, Paul M. 1986. Increasing Returns and Long-Run Growth. *Journal of Political Economy* 94(5): 1002–1037.

———. 1990. Endogenous Technological Change. *Journal of Political Economy* 98 (5) part 2:S71–S102.

Rothschild, Michael. 1990. *Bionomics*. New York: Henry Holt.

Ryan, Doris. 1991. RAPID/NM. Presentation at the Fourth Annual Workshop on Software Reuse, 18–22 November, Reston, Virginia.

Salin, Phil. 1990. The Ecology of Decisions, or, "An Inquiry into the Nature and Causes of the Wealth of Kitchens." *Market Process* 8:91–114.

Shina, Sammy. 1991. *Concurrent Engineering and Design for Manufacture of Electronics Products*. New York: Van Nostrand Reinhold.

Smith, Adam. 1976 [1776]. *An Inquiry Into the Nature and Causes of the Wealth of Nations*. Chicago: University of Chicago Press.

Smith, M. F. 1991. *Software Prototyping: Adoption, Practice, and Management*. London: McGraw-Hill.

Solow, Robert M. 1956. A Contribution to the Theory of Economic Growth, *Quarterly Journal of Economics* 70 (1):65–94.

———. 1970. *Growth Theory: an Exposition*. Oxford: Clarendon.

Sowell, Thomas. 1980. *Knowledge and Decisions*. New York: Basic Books.

Spurr, Kathy, and Paul Layzell, eds. 1992. *CASE, Current Practice, Future Prospects*. Chichester: Wiley.

Stiglitz, Joseph E. 1990. Comments: Some Retrospective Views on Growth Theory, in Diamond, Peter. *Growth/Productivity/Unemployment,* Cambridge, Mass.: MIT Press.

Suh, Nam. 1990. *The Principles of Design*. New York: Oxford University Press.

Taylor, David A. 1990. *Object-Oriented Technology: A Manager's Guide*. Alameda, Calif.: Servio Cororation

Tirso, Jesus. 1991. IBM Reuse Program. Presentation given at the Fourth Annual Workshop on Software Reuse, 18–22 November, Reston, Virginia.

Vaughn, Karen. 1990. The Mengerian Roots of the Austrian Revival. *History of Political Economy*. Supplemental issue.

Wheelwright, Steven C., and Kim B. Clark. 1992. *Revolutionizing Product Development*. New York: The Free Press.

Whitefield, Bob and Ken Auer. 1991. You can't do that in Smalltalk! Or Can You? *Object Magazine* 1 (May/June):64–69.

Womack, James P., Daniel T. Jones, and Daniel Roos. 1990. *The Machine that Changed the World.* New York: Harper Perennial.

INDEX

Abstract data type, 47, 106–107
Adams, Sam, 53, 80, 81, 90, 113–115
Agriculture, 17–19
Alcoa, 179
Allen, Peter, 92, 93–94
Assembly language, 35
Auer, Ken, 60–61
Austrian School of economics, 2n,
  7–8, 95, 166
Automatic programming, 41–42,
  75–78

Beck, Kent, 63, 82, 102–104
Bit rot, 23
Bosworth, George, 139, 140
Bridging the semantic gap, 38, 39, 80
Browsers, 41, 74
Bugs, 33
Built-in debugger, 72–73

C programs, 102
Capital accumulation, 166–170
Capital combinations, 168
Capital destruction, 174, 176
Capital equipment, 8–9
Capital goods, 34–42
  across time and space, 16–21, 147
  categories, 24–26
  complementarity, 21–23, 49n,
    166–170
  consumption goods and, 163
  defined, 3
  design, 27–28
  first order, 23
  as knowledge, 7–16
  orders, 23–24
  quantifiability of, 164–165
Capital maintenance, 22–23, 38, 95
Capital recombination, 94, 169

Capital stock, 165–166n
Capital structure, 21–27
  defined, 4
  as ecosystem, 92
  evolution, 3–7, 38
  lengthening, 23–24, 119–143,
    166–167
  social interaction in, 16–21
Capital value
  maintenance, 22–23, 89–90, 155
  measurement, 164–165
CASE tools, 37, 40, 66–71, 151, 153
  defined, 67–68
  functions, 69–71
Charge-per-use system, 128–131,
  133–134, 159
Class hierarchy browsers, 41
Classes, 41, 47–48, 83–84, 150, 155
COBOL, 174
Code applications, 127
Code dependability, 116
Code generators, 34, 41, 66, 69, 77
Code reuse, 112–113
Coevolutionary development, 91–92,
  155
Common Object Management
  Request Broker (CORBA),
  132
Communal property, 44n
Competition, 142, 160
Compilers, 34, 40, 66, 75
Complementarity
  among capital goods, 21–23,
    166–170
  ignored in growth theories,
    162, 174
  maintenance of, 38
  in modular programming, 33
  of software tools, 31, 38

189

IEEE

COMPUTER SOCIETY

Press Activities Board

IEEE Computer Society Publications

The world-renowned IEEE Computer Society publishes, promotes, and distributes a wide variety of authoritative computer science and engineering texts. These books are available from most retail outlets. The IEEE Computer Society is seeking new practitioner-oriented and leading-edge research titles in computer science and computer engineering. Visit the Online Catalog, http://computer.org, for a list of products and new author information.

Submission of proposals: For guidelines and information on the IEEE Computer Society books, send e-mail to cs.books@computer.org or write to the Project Editor, IEEE Computer Society, P.O. Box 3014, 10662 Los Vaqueros Circle, Los Alamitos, CA 90720-1314. Telephone +1 714-821-8380. FAX +1 714-761-1784.

IEEE Computer Society Proceedings

The IEEE Computer Society also produces and actively promotes the proceedings of more than 130 acclaimed international conferences each year in multimedia formats that include hard and softcover books, CD-ROMs, videos, and on-line publications.

For information on the IEEE Computer Society proceedings, send e-mail to cs.books@computer.org or write to Proceedings, IEEE Computer Society, P.O. Box 3014, 10662 Los Vaqueros Circle, Los Alamitos, CA 90720-1314. Telephone +1 714-821-8380. FAX +1 714-761-1784.

Additional information regarding the Computer Society, conferences and proceedings, CD-ROMs, videos, and books can also be accessed from our web site at http://computer.org/cspress